# PATHWAYS
## OF THE SOUL

# PATHWAYS
## OF THE SOUL

*Exploring the Human Journey*

Hillevi Ruumet, Ph.D.

Order this book online at www.trafford.com
or email orders@trafford.com

Most Trafford titles are also available at major online book retailers.

Print information available on the last page.

ISBN: 978-1-4120-9236-4 (sc)

*Trafford rev. 07/31/2018*

 www.trafford.com

**North America & international**
toll-free: 1 888 232 4444 (USA & Canada)
fax: 812 355 4082

# DEDICATION

For my children
and grandchildren
and their generations.

# CONTENTS

# AN INVITATION

I invite you to walk through some common pathways of your soul's human journey with me, not only with your mind, but also with your heart and your body. Think not just of the thoughts and images I will share with you, but how these live in and through you. We will have a general "map" to guide us, a "soul map" if you will, and we will walk through it together.

So far, the strongest response to my presentations of this "soul map" has come from men and women who are conscious seekers of wholeness and self-realization in some form. If it resonates with you, you may well resemble them in some or all of the following ways:

- You are open-minded and growth-oriented.
- You tend to be introspective and reflective.
- You have done a significant amount of inner work.
- You may have had some "psychic" or mystical experiences that you may or may not have understood at the time.
- Meaning and purpose in life are important to you.
- You are environmentally concerned and socially inclusive.
- You are capable of honest self-observation and laughing at your own foibles.

- You have an expansive and benevolent sense of humor.
- You tend to be spiritually exploratory and non-dogmatic.

We all basically want to be healthy, happy and, whether we call it that or not, holy. If we reject the "holy" part we may be forgetting its core meaning of "whole" and equating it with the "holier than thou" attitude we instinctively recoil from because it is really an ego trip. Or perhaps we think of holiness as far beyond us, belonging to spiritual giants and enlightened beings but not possible for us ordinary humans.

The "personal growth" books and workshops so popular in today's Western world mainly seek to cultivate the development of a well functioning, mature personality—as represented by the Adult self in Transactional Analysis, or the healthy human who is able to love and to work productively as described by Freud. This is certainly worthwhile in promoting our mental health and helping to move us toward personal wholeness. Yet there is much more to us, and the burgeoning interest in spirituality today shows that we are beginning to recognize that. We are not just personal, but *trans*personal, and this is the discovery the psycho-spiritual journey is ultimately about.

In essence, we are Spirit. This is our true identity and can never be lost, only obscured or forgotten. Spirit simply *is*, and there is nowhere and no thing It is not. The individually personified form of this divine energy is what we call "soul"— that is, embodied Spirit born into a specific time and place, into a specific matrix of family and society. We are en-*souled*, the holy meeting ground of Spirit and matter.

We each have our own way to wholeness—holiness—our unique way back to our home in Spirit, which our essence has never left. This journey takes us through the spiraling labyrinth of our individual lives, with many twists and turns, and occasional dead ends. Yet deep down our heart recognizes our authentic path when we encounter it, and then it becomes a matter of motivation and courage to commit to it and stay the course.

Some broad outlines of this psycho-spiritual growth process form the core of this book. If most or even all of the descriptors listed above fit you, what follows will help you understand where in your journey you may be now, where you have been, and where your path may take you next.

# THE CALL OF THE SEED

The emergence of this psycho-spiritual map was a surprise to me – like a sudden birth when I had no idea I was pregnant. It grew organically through several decades of psychotherapeutic practice and personal inner work, and felt like an energetic representation in my body – images intricate and rainbow-like, three-dimensional holograms in constant motion that somehow bypassed my intellect and intellectual labeling but guided my intuition to where something important was emerging for me or the person I was working with as a psychotherapist. I now like to think that some deep wisdom within sheltered it from conscious view until it was mature enough to stand up to my conceptual onslaughts.

Teaching this emerging "map" publicly was also unexpected, prompted in 1995 by my participation in a spiritual guidance class taught by a colleague at the Institute of Transpersonal Psychology in California, where I served on the core faculty. The students had been discussing two major developmental models and complaining that they were too "neat" and linear, so at one point I heard myself say, "Well, if you want a messy model, I have one for you." At that point, I inwardly kicked myself for opening my mouth, but they were intrigued, and the instructor asked if I would present my "messy model" at the next class session.

It was the first time I had tried to explain it in words, but to my surprise, as I started talking the words came easily. The response of the students was both thoughtful and enthusiastic, so I was invited to present the model more widely, and now, after ten years of discussion, refinement, and my own further travels along the pathways I describe, the results have found their way into expression through this book.

A flower does not strive to bloom. It does not worry about blooming, and it does not consult botanical experts about being a better bloomer. Nor does it ponder whether it should become a rose or a daisy. Given the right environment, it blooms naturally, and it blooms into the kind of flower its seed meant it to be. It blooms simply because that is the expression of its essence and being – just as it is ours to realize our true nature when inner and outer conditions align toward that outcome.

Buddhism speaks of this as interdependent co-arising, which means that things happen when both our intentions and habitual response patterns come together with outer circumstances and conditions which prompt them to manifest in particular ways. Hopefully, these will be benign and eventually facilitate our unique "blooming."

We know what some of these helpful conditions are, and what helps to create them. They are the underlying common substrate of all spiritual traditions, beyond their culturally conditioned institutional overlay. Silence. Ethical living. Self-understanding. Love. Empathy. Compassion. Taking time to attend to "the small, silent voice" inside, which tends to be audible only when we turn toward inward silence and are open to hearing it. Honoring incarnation in the form of the Earth and our own bodies. Protecting life in all its forms. Mindfulness. Weeding out unhelpful habits of thought and action. Excavating the deep roots of our neurotic patterns and clearing the boulders of trauma and fear that block our way. Most of all, turning our face often toward the sunlight of Spirit and tending the holy wherever we find it. Most of this also constitutes the substance of effective psychotherapy.

We do not grow into our fullness in a straight line. This is probably why the image of a spiral, or a labyrinth, is seen in almost all cultures as a metaphor for the spiritual journey. To see psychological or spiritual development as a straight hike up the proverbial mountain, and ourselves as striving ever upward over obstacles, stalwartly persevering and finally making it to the top, is appealingly heroic but much too neat for the interdependence, unpredictability, and serendipity of our actual lives. Think about it: Has your life ever moved neatly "onward and upward"? Mine certainly has not.

Wholeness as a multi-dimensional, creative, loving, and productive human being can be consciously worked toward and, at least in principle, achieved. Enlightenment is different. It is more like a butterfly that eludes us while we chase it, but briefly settles on our shoulder when we relax, put away the net, and simply open to the experience of the moment – and then it flies away again. There is nothing we can do to *make* it happen, and our ambitious, self-absorbed "little me" – Ego – hates that.

Yes, we *are* Spirit. But we are *embodied* Spirit, and many of us have difficulty seeing and fully accepting the need to integrate our mental/physical/emotional/spiritual aspects into a balanced and functionally harmonious whole. Or, seeing the need, we may doubt whether it is really possible, or at least possible for *us*. Through cultivated awareness, introspection, and self-mastery, however, we can strive toward personal wholeness in ways we cannot strive to be enlightened, because, as all the spiritual traditions tell us, that ultimate state cannot be reached by the Ego. Enlightenment transcends Ego, and the more we try to grasp it, the more enlightenment eludes us. Ego, as such, cannot be enlightened.

That said, it is also true that a more spacious, clear mind and open heart provide more openings for light of Spirit to spontaneously shine through. Joseph Campbell liked to point out that we are always (in all ways) potentially "transparent to transcendence." A nun who taught me spiritual direction liked to say that we are "marinated in God," whether aware of it or not. The veil between God and us can lift anywhere, at any time, for a moment or longer, and in rare cases even permanently.

We must negotiate life's highways and by-ways in any case, and having a conceptual "map" that makes sense of our actual experience can help us navigate with a greater sense of purpose and direction. This is not to suggest a grim journey, marching stoically toward a pre-determined destination, or the map as a directive to stick to its delineated pathways, but rather an invitation to dance down the path. We can think of it as dancing with life in a way that harmonizes body, spirit, and psyche into an integral whole – a "soul dance," if you will, with basic steps to adapt into our own forms.

This sounds simple, but for most of us, doing it is far more complex, and our minds can create endless complications along the way. We embark on our human journey with no given roadmap except our biological inheritance and those traditional teachings our ancestors and teachers passed on to us as guidelines. All may carry their own deep truth, but they also largely reflect the experiences, mythologies, and prejudices of earlier times and context. That leaves us with the task of wisely discerning the timeless within the time-bound. A frequent guiding premise for such discernment is that the longer something endures as a basic truth, while still maintaining its vitality and capacity to help us mature as human beings through successive generations and across cultures, the more likely it is to be in the timeless category.

I think of our soul dance as a spiraling process unfolding

along two axes, one evolving vertically in fairly predictable stages toward ever greater spiritual insight and recognition of ultimate reality, and the other axis deepening and extending our experience horizontally as well-rounded human beings within the context of our particular home Center in all its breadth and diversity. This is a very ancient dance, arising somewhere in the mysterious dawn of human history and encompassing both height and depth, both the psychological and the spiritual – from incarnation and birth to death, then dissolution once more into Spirit, ready for an invitation to another dance.

Psychological development alone, without the spiritual dimension, ultimately reaches a deflated dead end, with fallout in frustration, stress, anxiety, depression, and addiction. On the other hand, exclusive emphasis on the spiritual without concomitant psychological development can lead to "shadow" eruptions, that is, disowned and unlived parts of the psyche manifesting in dysfunctional and even destructive ways. Examples of such eruptions may be the phenomena of well known Christian preachers becoming involved in scandals, or Eastern spiritual teachers coming to the West and getting into similar trouble, almost always over issues involving money, sex, and/or power. These relate to Centers ONE, TWO, and THREE, respectively, which will be described and discussed in the chapters that follow.

Every model of how things are is a myth, in Joseph Campbell's sense of the word, describing a collective soul story "writ large" and reflecting the inner life of a particular human era, culture, and stage of development. In this sense of the term, the spiraling map that I will outline here is also mythical, as are all conceptual models of the human journey, inner and/or outer. The perception of truth in a myth depends on its experienced resonance with the particular time, culture, and psychology that it expresses, though there are core themes that recur in similar forms cross-culturally and across time.

Because these perennial themes arise from core experiences of our human condition which we all share, they are in their essence universal, though manifesting in different variations. Jungian psychology describes these as archetypal patterns derived from primordial tendencies for human experience to cluster around certain emotionally charged symbols and images, frequently personified as gods and goddesses, superhuman heroes and heroines, and other transcendent beings.

When we connect with a myth or archetypal image, it brings new energy and meaning into our lives at times when we feel we are merely "treading water," "going through the motions," or "burning out." It can function as an inner call to something new. This something may be quite nebulous and feel strange or even impossible, perhaps a stretch of our capacities we are not sure we can manage, but it comes from deep within, like a sprouting urge of the seed potentials we were born with but which are still dormant. The dormancy may have come about for sound practical reasons. Perhaps the business of life, work, and/or family has demanded all our time and commitment, sparing little energy to think about personal growth. But it is the seed's nature to seek growth nonetheless.

The idea of the seed is not new. The poet Rumi says that each of us has a duty to perform in this life, and if we do not find what it is and do it, we will have wasted our lives. In his book *The Soul Code*, James Hillman expands on a similar idea. He says we are each an acorn which is meant to grow into its unique tree-ness, and throughout our lives, there is something in us that keeps pulling toward living the fullness of that form. Until we answer that call, we remain inwardly restless and unfulfilled.

The call of the seed is always toward the unknown, and that can be frightening. We don't know what the seed will look like fully grown, or even if it will survive to maturity. I have felt a little like that about this book, since every developmental model also reflects the personal mythology of its author – inevitably, because we speak most authentically when we speak from our own experience. Yet, when seen clearly enough, what is deeply human in any one of us abuts the universal.

# CHAPTER ONE

# NOURISHING THE SEED

Nobody has ever walked into my office saying, "My ego is too big. Please help me shrink it." Perhaps someone has made that perceptive self-diagnosis somewhere, but in any event, something has to "pinch" the psyche to prompt the call for an appointment. With very few exceptions, we are motivated to seek psychotherapy and go to personal growth workshops by emotional and interpersonal pain, because we feel a need to change something in our lives. When we are happy and everything is going well, we have no impetus to seek change.

As I worked with people over the years on a wide variety of issues, I noticed that although human problems in general tend to fall into similar categories, the particulars are always unique. There is a potential novel in every life. The perspective of the person presenting the problem, and the capacity to dis-identify from the problem sufficiently to consider alternative meanings and solutions, likewise varied enormously. Solutions therefore had to arise out of the person's own psychological landscape, making each necessarily different.

The ability to objectively self-witness rather than be submerged in their problems turned out to be a critical difference between those who truly grew through psycho-therapy and those who just managed to patch up the presenting problem sufficiently to get back to business as usual. The latter gained enough knowledge and/or skills to improve their everyday lives and carry on as before. This is fine as a temporary solution, but it sets up conditions for similar problems to recur in the future. I always wondered why so many people settled for this when more was possible.

Being so interested myself in growth and transformation, and being the sort of person who values explanatory paradigms that make sense to me, even if only provisionally, I was challenged and intrigued by these differences in goals and motivation. I looked for guidance from existing theories of development, and each provided a piece of the puzzle, but I still lacked an overarching conceptual model to fit them all together.

C.G. Jung provided the biggest piece, and his work became the basic integrative umbrella for my teaching and therapeutic work for many years. It also became a bridge for me from Psyche to Spirit, and the interaction of these two aspects in our growth process became a central focus for my work and personal development. This became the context of my practice as a therapist as I tried to connect with each person wherever they were in their process.

Then, in the seventies, I discovered the work of Ken Wilber, and his chakra-based "spectrum psychology" model of human development was an epiphany for me. Had it been formulated then as it is now, it might have become a comfortable theoretical framework for me to settle into, but as articulated at that time, I found it less helpful than I had hoped when I tried to translate it into the unpredictable convolutions of everyday life. My own development felt much more like a spiral or labyrinth than a neat progression of linear stages, and this also seemed true of the people I worked with as a therapist.

A casual mealtime conversation with the late Joseph Campbell serendipitously provided the seminal image for my own psycho-spiritual growth "map." I shared with him my admiration in theory and frustration in practice with Wilber's model. I told him that my own experience was more spiral-like than an orderly progression up the chakras. "Oh, yes," he said, "it is more like *this*," and asked for a pen. He drew the diagram in Figure 1 on a napkin, to which I responded with an immediate visceral sense of "Yes!" – like spinning mental tumblers clicking into place. I recognized it as an invaluable gift to my understanding as well as validation of my own sense of inner movement, but did not think to ask him about the specific source of his diagram. I now wish I had.

Though still too neat to fit what I was seeing and experiencing in my daily life and work, this rudimentary diagram worked pretty well, and I was able to get more and more useful guidance from it in working with people, especially those for whom the interplay of the psychological and the spiritual was at the heart of their growth process. It was through their experiences, as well as that of friends and my own, that the model presented here took form. In Hindu imagery, it felt like the dance of Shiva and Shakti: Shiva as the form, Shakti as the dancing divine energy, and I as a resonator trying to follow and align with the process, always trying to discern a higher wisdom in whatever form it chose to manifest.

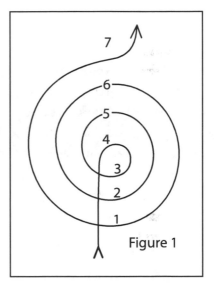

Figure 1

This is the birth story of my "messy model" of psycho-spiritual development, which highlights the general paths and mindscapes we all travel through as we develop psychologically and spiritually. It is basically a "voice from the trenches" of human struggle toward wholeness and self-realization rather than an academic theory: an outline of experiential way-finding as we wend our way through the uncharted territories of our individual lives. Many elegant theories exist, and I admire them. As a piece of the overall conceptual mosaic of human development, this model, too, may bring its own light and clarity to whoever might benefit from it.

## Brief Overview of the Seven Centers

The broad spans and cycles of psycho-spiritual development delineated in this book are oriented around seven Centers analogous to the chakras of Eastern symbology, each representing a span of consciousness with central developmental tasks, challenges, obstacles, and maturational fruits associated with it. These Centers will be discussed in detail through the chapters that follow. I am using a seven-chakra framework because it is the one most commonly known, although there are alternative systems which differ from it somewhat. A simplified depiction of my model as it has evolved to date is shown in Figure 2 on the following page. Briefly, as suggested by the images in the diagram, each Center has a basic goal, which in its healthy form furthers growth, expansiveness and evolution, and in its unhealthy form leads to contraction and fear of what lies beyond our habituated comfort zone. This latter seems to be the default program if the growth challenges of each Center are not actively engaged and mastered, and leads to unhelpful forms of adaptation that become entrenched as obstacles to further development.

The Centers are quite fluid and over-lapping, so there are no neat boundaries between them, yet there are distinct differences among them in their typical world-view and

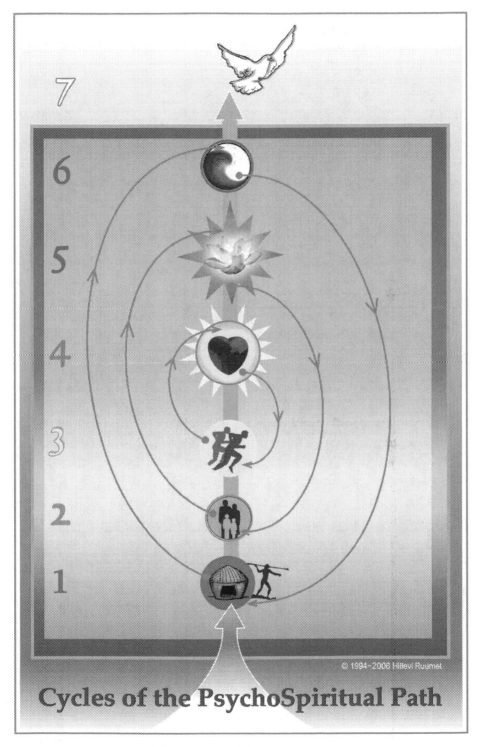

Cycles of the PsychoSpiritual Path

© 1994–2006 Hillevi Ruumet

experience of self in relation to the outer world.

What follows are distilled descriptors of both fruitful and stagnant outcomes:

| | Healthy Outcome | Unhealthy Outcome |
|---|---|---|
| *Center 1:* | Good survival skills | Fearful vigilance |
| *Center 2:* | Positive relational/sexual self-image | Social and self-alienation |
| *Center 3:* | Competence and/or mastery in some area of productive activity | Inadequacy, often masked by an inflated ego |
| *Center 4:* | Empathy and inclusiveness | Attachment to own reference group, rejection of others |
| *Center 5:* | Creative self-expression | Indulgent self-display |
| *Center 6:* | Wisdom, mind/body harmony | Rigidity, intellectualization, dogmatism |
| *Center 7:* | Enlightened mind, expressed through wise, compassionate action in the world | Pseudo-spirituality, or narrow religiosity and/or ungrounded "transcendence" |

Spiritual and psychological growth interweave as warp and woof in the weaving of our lives. Without both, the fabric cannot hold together, although it can survive some flaws and "holes," because these are fixable. The described patterns of psychological and spiritual movement through and among the Centers constitute a general, simplified "superhighway" map only, with the actual back roads and byways traveled day to day forming the living web that connects and weaves through them all. No generalized model can accurately describe the infinite variations of individual experience. Exploration of our own paths is up to us, though knowing our ultimate direction helps set the course.

I chose to use the term "Centers" rather than "chakras" for each span of consciousness we grow through in order to focus on the developmental tasks and characteristics symbolically related to the various energies rather than the energies themselves, all of which belong to our life processes. These energies are active and potentially available at all stages of our development, though of varying intensity in any given context and in any given person. I will not focus on them as such in this book, but rather on the progressive phases of psycho-spiritual development which tend to maintain certain characteristics over substantial periods of time, and hence act as a kind of "center of gravity" or "home base" for the total personality, each at a particular stage of the journey.

It is in the service of our home Center's goals and purposes that we use the energies of all the chakras, and it is in the consensual language and concepts of its worldview that we interpret our experiences. Each Center with its span of consciousness and understanding has certain boundaries and perceptual biases, with each successive Center expanding those boundaries more and more toward an ultimately unbounded view.

While the energies of the chakras are constantly moving and interacting kaleidoscopically, the Centers are much more stable. Some people spend a whole lifetime mostly deepening and expanding their experience of just one Center, using the energies of the other Centers in support of that. Other people seem to be born with a life trajectory, and head toward a target Center as soon as possible after the necessary and sometimes minimal development of the foundational Centers. Mozart may be a historical case in point, as might other more contemporary prodigies and geniuses. In these cases, the urgency of the acorn's drive to manifest its tree-ness seems unusually clear.

It is more common, however, to move our center of gravity permanently from one Center to another (if indeed we do) over the course of many years or a lifetime – some might say lifetimes. Such a move is transformational, and entails major shifts in consciousness. The expanded worldview resulting from this requires a total realignment of all our conceptual categories, guiding mythologies – and neuroses. A genuine transformation of this kind does not involve rejecting or de-valuing preceding home Centers, only relativizing them. Some things are left behind, some are refurbished to fit the space of our new "home."

Our span of consciousness expands with a move from one Center to the next but includes all that has been learned at the previous stages, at best as fruits capable of seeding further growth, at worst as "trailers of unfinished business" that will create obstacles on our path. Since we all acquire both gifts and trailers as we develop, and never actualize all of our potentials at any given stage, we always have inner work to do, which we can either embrace or refuse. If refused, however, these trailers hang around, draining energy and distorting our perception, especially if we are not aware of them, or persist in denying or ignoring them.

Those of us who consciously aspire to become mature, integral human beings cannot refuse to deal with these developmental issues and still make authentic progress on our psycho-spiritual path. What has not been learned or integrated, or has been learned in a hurtful way, becomes "shadow" baggage that will tend to undermine the usefulness of the gifts of whatever Center the baggage belongs to, and will have to be dealt with at some point if we are not to suffer developmental arrest.

What this means is that whatever in ourselves we have disowned or never known consciously is buried in the unconscious, in the darkness of shadow rather than being visible in the light of awareness. Our reasons for relegating something to "shadow," even positive potentials and qualities, may have been a valid childhood response to environmental conditions, but that does not make it go away. Like a mischievous child who is ignored or excessively restricted, the suppressed part of us may act out unpredictably, often in embarrassing or even destructive ways.

Not everyone is impelled to do the whole journey. That drive seems to depend on individual motivation, opportunity, and inherent predilection. It is possible to lead a full and productive life without ever seeing any need for an inner journey, or even being exposed to the possibility, but once "invited" to the dance of becoming, refusal is not a fruitful option. Our best choice then is to accept graciously and dance consciously, know how and why we are doing it, and find joy in the process.

We do not move directly or smoothly from one Center to the next. We wander in what ultimately feels like a spiral with an unobstructed path leading us through, but in the walking it seems more like a convoluted maze. We see our path clearly only in hindsight, when we may refer to it as "my Path," "what I was meant to do," or on a grander scale, "my destiny" or "God's Will." Each of us must find it for ourselves. The symbols and images that arise and give meaning to our experience of the different Centers are also very personal, as well as reflecting our particular life experiences and family spiritual traditions. I also invite you to explore these as we go along, and discern how they can best serve you.

To graphically show the return cycles, I chose to present the model vertically, but you can also picture it as concentric circles representing expanding spans of consciousness, with boundaries at each stage becoming more and more trans-lucent until they finally become totally clear, with no boundaries at all. Ultimately, of course, the mystical traditions tell us there is no path, no journey, and even no separate traveler. We are already Home. But we have to walk the walk to that final realization. Conceptual understanding alone will not help. It has to be an embodied experience, beyond concepts, involving heart, mind, body, and spirit.

## Some Broad Distinctions

In dividing the Centers into two broad categories, I borrow again from Joseph Campbell. At a workshop in Hawaii in 1983, he spoke of two kinds of people. He called "in-laws" those of us whose world is defined by the consensus reality of our culture, and who live comfortably within these "laws" of our cultural conditioning without any strong impetus to question or move beyond them. In my model these would be inhabitants of Centers ONE, TWO, and THREE as home base, and stretch into FOUR as what I am calling the "humanistic bulge" (to be explained later). Like fish so totally at home in water that they do not realize it exists as such, we take our conditioned reality for granted as *the* obvious and only reality.

The "out-laws" are those whose perceived reality and experiences spill over the boundaries of these collective "laws" into a larger view, and who therefore feel impelled to question and often challenge the assumptions and beliefs of their culture. As "out-laws," we are the world's "seekers" and pushers of conventional envelopes, whether explicitly "spiritual" or not. Out-laws are, by definition, a minority, but they are necessary channels and catalysts for the life-stream of human evolution. The impulse and curiosity to explore beyond the "water" of our foundational Centers' reality usually arises within the span of Center FOUR, but most often really takes off when the Star of Center FIVE starts beckoning to us in a way we can't ignore. What I mean by this will become clear as we go along.

This model will be most helpful to "out-laws," whether self-identified as such or not. Conventional psychology does a fine job of describing "in-law" development, and I do not aspire to add to that abundant literature. However, the fact that you are interested in this book may well brand you as an "out-law," or someone on the brink of expanding the boundaries of your "in-law" mindscape. If so, I believe you will respond to the chapters on the "Aloha Waltz" and/or the "Descent Tango" in particular with a rueful sense of recognition.

There is no such thing as a purely spiritual center, though Center SEVEN holds that place in the context of this model. Spirit is actually the ground and context of everything, but its specific form of expression varies not only from person to person but also in fairly predictable ways from Center to Center. Also, different cultures form different spiritual and religious traditions, and these traditions in turn shape social structures and worldviews, including religious institutions and their formal belief systems.

In normal development, we all become children of our cultural conditioning, like the proverbial fish. To see "water" would posit something that is not water, inconceivable from this perspective. Even if we notice something strange happening near the surface when raindrops create unusual round designs we don't usually see, we may stifle our curiosity about it in deference to what our elders have taught us. But what if one day, playfully or unwittingly, we break through the surface into the air above, catching glimpses of an inconceivably vast, non-liquid expanse, and suddenly realize there is a whole world beyond water?

Now we have a problem. Do we pretend we didn't see what we saw? Do we treat it as a mirage – "only my imagination"? Do we say that it cannot exist because that is what our fish elders have taught us? Or do we approach it, with some trepidation perhaps, as something we need to understand?

Ignore or explore? This is now a choice that will determine our future. Many of us have faced this kind of decision point in our lives, and it is not easy, especially where the "in-law" culture demands conformity, and the price of challenging and/or transgressing its norms can be severe. We can all think of well-known historical and contemporary examples of people who push the edge of accepted "reality" beyond a certain point and are at best seen as misfits or weirdoes, and at worst ostracized, persecuted, or even killed.

Young people, and especially children, often have mystical and transpersonal experiences that they keep secret, like seeing "angels," or seeing colors around people, or having accurate premonitions. This secrecy usually reflects fear of adult ridicule or even punishment, which means they have already internalized the boundaries of permissible perceptions. They themselves may also find such experiences strange or frightening.

On the other hand, these experiences may feel exciting and desirable, taking them into a dreamlike world beyond an everyday life they may find difficult or boring. Some may seek this through drugs – and find a nightmare instead. Perhaps if we taught our young more about the workings and capacities of the human mind, and accepted whatever they experience as something to explore and learn from rather than reject, they would learn to be more aware of their own inner depth and explore such experiences in a healthy way, hopefully with someone qualified to support and guide them.

However it happens, once we have seen beyond what we considered the limits of "reality" and own what we have seen, there is no way to authentically go back. We do not necessarily *choose* to become more conscious. Some of us are dragged, kicking and screaming, by unexpected experiences positive *or* negative that challenge our traditional assumptions. Some say that all addictions are a misdirected search for spiritual experience, which is interesting in the context of our contemporary world with its epidemic of addictions in all imaginable forms.

Exploration can be uncomfortable and even risky, but, for better or worse, we cannot "un-eat" the proverbial apple. We cannot restore lost innocence – or ignorance. Struggling to do so is ultimately counterproductive. We can seek to suppress what we have seen, and try to deny having seen it. We can act like frightened fish and "swim" into the depths, as far as possible from the surface, but we always know a much more spacious reality is there, hovering above our heads, a nagging invitation to evolution and liberation from our self-imposed limitations. So we might as well open ourselves to seeing our world as clearly as we can, with all the integrity, discernment, and compassion toward ourselves that we can muster.

### Some Caveats

It would be wise, as you read on, to not make these Centers as described into competitive "milestones," or into a measure of how "evolved" (or not) you are spiritually or psychologically, and least of all to compare yourself with or judge others. First of all, we have no way of reliably knowing from outer observation who is or is not more or less evolved, or whether they are making "progress." Spiritual teachers of all traditions warn us that a competitive or judgmental attitude is a major obstacle to authentic spiritual maturation. We can only step forward from where we are at the moment; we can only broaden our span of consciousness from what it is right now; the only path we can tread is the one we are actually walking.

While our pivotal growth tasks seem to cluster around one or two Centers, our focus may be in different places at different times, in different aspects of our lives, or in different components of our personality. Some parts of us are wiser than others, and our inner "cast of characters" may be dealing with a variety of issues all over the psycho-spiritual map. Yet we all remain embedded in Spirit and have the potential to recognize It at any time. Spirit is always living through us. Our essence is transpersonal even as its expression is personal and always changing.

It is healthy to embrace (with discernment, of course) whatever form of spirituality feels like home at any stage of life, even if it may later change in ways we cannot currently foresee. As we move from one Center to another, our spiritual expression is also likely to take on the qualities and forms of practice of that Center. This can lead to confusion, but it can also lead to a rich synergy, depending on our attitude and understanding.

We can only move forward from where we are. Ultimate aspirations – such as wholeness, transcendence, enlightenment – are fine, but for the here and now, let's keep our reach within our grasp while at the same time extending our aspiration a bit beyond it. It is therefore best that each of us focus on the task at hand while also remaining aware of the ever-presence of the ultimate Ground of Being throughout our human journey.

If we think of this Ground, or Spirit, as the infinite space in which the book we hold in our hands rests, we will realize that to touch *It* (however we imagine and by whatever name we call *It*), all we need to do is pierce through the paper or simply shift our gaze into the endless space beyond. We all do this at times, however briefly and perhaps without recognizing what we are doing. Perhaps the most common such experience is when we totally lose ourselves in what has been called a "flow" experience, whether in creating art, or doing something physical we love and are good at, or work we are passionate about, or music, or beauty, or making love – or simply gazing at the boundless, clear sky.

Sages, saints, and spiritual masters live from this spaciousness, and that is ultimately what we are called to do, too. But first, and mindfully, we must accept the invitation to the journey of becoming what we seek.

# CHAPTER TWO

# THE JOURNEY BEGINS

## *Centers ONE and TWO: Need, Greed, and Cathexis*

Some years ago, there was a TV show called *This Is Your Life*. Various people were chosen to re-live their lives as reflected through the perceptions and memories of their significant others. There were surprise visits by people from the past they may not have seen for decades, even since early childhood, accompanied by visual and verbal snapshots of their major life events. The "stars" did not know who would show up or what would be recalled of their past, so the reactions were spontaneous and often moving. Sort of an intimate surprise party with an audience of millions.

As you read through the descriptions of the Centers, you might think of yourself as the sole guest and audience at a review of your own life, starting from its beginnings, and welcome whatever pops up on stage. Many of us know a lot about psychology and developmental theories, so the description of the foundational Centers (ONE, TWO, and THREE) will not be new. We have all lived within this matrix, and still do. It is our social and cultural context even if we as individuals have gone beyond it, and it is quite enlightening to take another look at the pathways we have walked so far from this broader perspective.

As we are formed by these foundational Centers, we acquire an inner "cast of characters" who will seem to be the protagonists of our life drama. There have been many ways of speaking of such characters in general terms, though in each of us they take a distinct and unique form: inner child (the part of us that never grew up, and retains both childhood innocence and childhood pain)), inner critic (the one who always chastises us for not measuring up in some way), inner parent (who may console us or tell us what to do, or sound very much like the critic), the professional, the rebel, the seeker, etc. These personified images tend to remain with us as we move through the various Centers, although they will hopefully mature and become integrated into our life drama. We may not like them all, but to the extent that we experience them as parts of ourselves, we have to deal with them and seek to be at peace with them. If we don't, they can become real troublemakers.

For many years, I had a bag lady living in my Survival Center (ONE). I say "had" because I haven't heard from her for several years now, so I assume she is gone or has morphed into something else. She was very real, though, and may still be hanging around in the wings ready to rush on-stage if or when life provides a sufficiently powerful cue. Whether I call her a "sub-personality" or a "personified complex," the fact remains that she was there and would kick up a big fuss every time my sense of basic security was threatened.

Wishing her away didn't work; she simply went underground and caused more mischief. Neither denial nor ignoring her did much good. So, realizing that I came by her honestly as a little child in the midst of World War II in Europe, experiencing hunger and homelessness in a chaotic world I was much too young to understand, I decided to accept and care for her as best I could. In fact, I bought her a station wagon and made sure that with the back seat down there was enough room in the back to sleep comfortably – just in case! My children, knowing that I am in no sense a camper, found this quite amusing, but to the bag lady it was comforting.  Ten years later, the car was unexpectedly totaled – and I never did get to sleep in it.  My new vehicle is much smaller, with no sleeping space.  So far, no objection from the bag lady.

Of course, "bag lady" or "hobo" reactions, which many people have told me they identify with, do have a powerful root in reality, which may account for the broad popular fascination with TV shows such as *Survivor*, or the Tom Hanks movie *Castaway*.  How many of us, as individuals, would be confident in our ability to survive if stranded in the wilderness alone without any of our technological accoutrements?  Or homeless on friendless city streets, for that matter?

Some of the following questions might help you track your own movement through each of the three foundational Centers as you re-visit your life up to the present.  You don't have to answer them right now.  Keep them in mind and reflect on them as you read along whenever it feels right.
  • What aspects of your personality have been developed and fully lived – or not?  Skills mastered or not?  For example, my bag lady reflects my lack of confidence in dealing with the practical realities of physical sustenance and self-support.
  • What has been difficult, passed through with little development, bypassed in order to get to something easier or more interesting, or relegated to someone else in your life to do for you?  For example, people with a "bag lady" or "hobo" living in their psyche may tend to hook up with life partners they expect to shoulder these survival tasks, or else become stoically independent.

• In your particular life drama, which "sub-personalities" of your inner "cast of characters" live at each Center? Has that changed over time? Can you give them names? What role have they played? Have the actual characters changed? If so, how?

• What would you say are your major inner obstacles to fulfilling your inherent potential?

The essential tasks, challenges, values, and gifts of the first two Centers, which we now turn to, are the basis for our development into healthy human adults. They form our foundational psycho-social matrix, however diverse in specific cultural values and forms the specific "in-law" worlds we grew up in might have been.

## The Foundational Matrix
## Center ONE: The Physical/Survival Center

From the original security of oneness with mother, we were thrust into a strange world with chaotic multi-sensory input. Depending on how difficult the birth was, how serene the setting, and how readily the nursing/nurturing connection with a mothering person was established, this left a deep impression, imprinting in us a global, visceral sense of this new environment as safe or threatening, friendly or hostile, trustworthy or unreliable. Our inarticulate responses might have ranged from pleasurable interest and curiosity to overwhelm and even terror.

Center ONE concerns the satisfaction of basic physical needs in the service of safety and survival. In talking about the hierarchy of needs, developmental psychology pioneer Abraham Maslow affirmed that "man's higher nature rests upon man's lower nature, needing it as a foundation and collapsing without this foundation."

Assuming all went well, we learned to live comfortably in a physical body, which we learned to call by a given name and distinguish from the rest of our still unfamiliar world. We learned to also name and relate to other people, starting with our caretakers. We progressively learned to do things for ourselves, feeling pleasure in our senses and the use of our growing physical skills. We found comfort in human touch and the nourishment we received from our mother or surrogate. We did not consciously know that all this was in the service of our safety and survival, but our instincts propelled us toward that end.

Largely through play as we grew increasingly mobile and able to manipulate our environment, we developed joy and delight in our physical abilities, in games and sports, and in making things with our hands. This taught us rudimentary practical skills and instilled a growing feeling of confidence in our ability to care for our own physical needs – a confidence that would sustain us throughout life.

If all this did not happen adequately because outer conditions such as poverty, ill health, parental neglect or criticism, a physical handicap, or even abuse, violence or war, instilled insecurity and fear rather than courage and confidence, we were left with growth tasks to take up in the future. Failing that, we might try the negative route of compensating for the lack of Center ONE development by using raw force to induce others to secure our safety and material well being for us.

Nevertheless, we developed a sense of ourselves as separate from our environment and we learned that, to a greater or lesser degree, we could voluntarily have an effect on the world around us. In response to having our needs met, we developed a deep attachment to those people and things we learned to identify as "my" or "mine." This kind of emotional attachment, in which we invest our energy in and identify with a person or any other cherished "object" outside ourselves, is well described by the psychoanalytic term "cathexis." It is a word that sounds like what it describes: a sticky, velcro-like, dependent attachment we learn to call "love." I like to use this word in connection with Centers ONE and TWO because it does not describe mature or unconditional love, and the distinction is important because mistaking "cathexis" for love as adults causes so many relationship problems.

I discuss both Centers together because at this stage they are fused. Babies need nurturing or they die, and as adults, when we are pulled back emotionally into these Centers by traumatic events, or during the "return cycles" we will talk about, our reaction may be based on this emotional fusion even though it is no longer rationally relevant. This may largely explain why otherwise well-functioning adults may stay in unhealthy relationships as though they had no choice, when it is clear to any objective observer that they do.

Because early cathectic attachment between mother and child (whether the biological mother or another caregiver) is in fact a matter of life and death for the baby, desperate clinging in adulthood to a person we feel dependent upon can feel like that as well. We never fully leave the emotional matrix into which we were born, and so abandonment can, to the infant still alive in the first two Centers within us, feel like a death sentence, in spite of a rational recognition otherwise. Consider the extreme emotional reactions so often seen in divorce cases where one spouse leaves and the one left feels as though facing death. Or in other situations perceived as abandonment when, even as well-functioning adults, we may similarly react with panic, as though we were left totally helpless and unable to take care of ourselves. Abandonment and fear of abandonment form a deep-seated emotional trigger that tends to hit us hard at the ONE or TWO level when activated, bypassing and even subverting the rational superstructure we have carefully constructed on our way to adulthood.

To the extent that we can recognize the legitimate origins of this once appropriate but now dysfunctional reaction, we will be able to respond to these situations in a more realistic way. Almost all of us have "trailers" or "sub-personalities" still active in our Survival Center, especially since most of us born and raised in highly urbanized, industrially developed countries have never learned to fend for ourselves in the raw physical world. These trailers are reflected in such characters as my bag lady, waiting to reappear in our inner drama.

At this stage of our development, and in those societies based in Center ONE, we relate to God, gods, or spirits in personified form, as all-powerful objective entities to be feared and propitiated lest they show their displeasure by harming us. We learn to do what appears to bring good fortune and divine blessings, or at least to fend off misfortune. Such conciliatory rituals are the origins of what we now dismiss as superstitions. We may feel we have evolved beyond them, but if we look closely, we see the reaction patterns of Center ONE still operating in our "modern" psyche and surfacing when our survival is threatened – or when we feel it is.

This was dramatically illustrated in our collective response to the attack of 9/11. A country firmly anchored in Center THREE, having been attacked in a shockingly unexpected and violent manner, immediately slid into the polarized "we/ they" mode of Center TWO and the aggressive territorial offense/defense stance of Center ONE. We all felt under threat and afraid, and this elicited an automatic, visceral Survival Center response in our leadership and the majority of the population. It just expressed itself through modern means and modern symbology. This is not a statement about the appropriateness or inappropriateness of the specific response as such, but simply to point out how we as a nation collectively reflected this primal pattern.

Some examples of what lengths we are capable of going to meet perceived threats to "me and mine" by a threatening "they" are also seen in the ugly phenomenon of "ethnic cleansing" in various parts of the world, as well as in the resurgence of militant fundamentalism (a regressive Center TWO reaction). The latter uses its self-serving interpretations of "God's Will" to justify all kinds of violence, often in the guise of helping, or wreaking divine revenge upon the "heathen" or "infidel" or "terrorist," or whoever is the current "bad guy" (depending on who is labeling whom).

Yet the sunny side of this Center, which is fundamentally driven by the pleasure/pain principle (seeking pleasure and avoiding pain), is childlike delight and pleasure in our senses through exploration and play – a zest for living described in French as "élan vital." I call it the vital self, and it is the healthy fruit of good First Center development, commonly seen in young children but not so often in modern adults.

Earth is our material (maternal) home, from which we were formed and to which our bodies will ultimately return. Our ancestors recognized this and honored her as Mother Earth, but we have been disregarding her in our collective ego inflation, and the consequences are beginning to make themselves felt. Fundamentally, Center ONE is for our grounding – rootedness in the earth, in our bodies, in our environment. If this does not happen, or happens insufficiently, we will have difficulty feeling secure in our bodies and in our world. No matter how accomplished in other ways we may become, we will have difficulty developing a mature, integrated personality, and trailers from this insufficiency will inevitably make themselves felt in situations calling for such maturity.

The point where this has to be most seriously addressed will come when we are pulled into the SIX-ONE return cycle (the Sophia Task). But we will talk about that later. The essential point to absorb here is that we must solidly walk on this earth regardless of what else we do, or continue to stumble in ways large and small. This is fundamental, and our highly technological culture is not designed to support this Center's full development. In fact, it mitigates against it and tends to devalue those who primarily excel here.

To help you reflect on how the Survival Center fits into your life, you might contemplate the following questions:

• Who (in the form of a "sub-personality" such as my bag lady) lives, or has lived, in your Survival Center?

• Are you prone to physical fear? What are you most afraid of?

• How do you protect yourself when you go into survival mode? If you withdraw, what is your "turtle shell" made of? If you fight, what is your weapon?

• Do you feel at home in your body? Do you take good care of your physical health?

• Do you feel confident in your ability to deal with the material world?

• How do you play? Do you?

• What superstitions still influence you at vulnerable times?

• Did you, as you grew up, bring with you the gift of a grounded, confident "vital self" as a fruit of Center ONE, ready to tackle the work of the world and the challenges of adulthood? If not, what might help it develop now?

## "Fortress We"
## Center TWO: The Emotional/Kinship Center

This Center also kicks in at birth, and is primarily focused on need, greed, and cathexis (dependent emotional attachment). It refers to the social matrix that receives us and cares for us when we are born, and without which we cannot survive. The first instinctive movement of a newborn is to turn its head in search of the nipple nature has programmed it to look for. To have that source of nourishment be there at that time is our most urgent and basic need, and we quickly cathect the source of its fulfillment. This is part of the mammalian heritage that we share with other species in immediate need of physical mothering.

If our needs are not adequately met, greed later develops as an effort to grasp and hoard scarce supplies, creating a fear of lack and a diffuse insecurity which later makes learning to share with others a challenge. Control issues originate here as well, as we strive to satisfy our needs by manipulating the environment and the people around us.

Often, we serve our greed in the guise of need. If we are lucky enough to be well nurtured and positively mirrored by our parents or surrogates, we learn to interact in ways that give us a sense of belonging and well being, which in turn opens us to the development of generosity.

Central to our development at Center TWO is the need to be loved and cared for, to belong, and to be accepted by our family and later our extended kinship circle. We develop social skills that elicit the responses we seek, whether by crying or (later) being intentionally cute, or (even later) developing an affable social persona. Our security in being cared for enables us to develop basic visceral acceptance of the world and a feeling of "I'm OK" which in time expands to "You're OK too," at least within the kinship circle we learn to identify with as "we." The "they" who are not part of the "we" circle are a bit suspect at first, but in a benign environment we can also learn to expand our circle of care bit by bit. Our "we" circle is very small to begin with, but in healthy development it will grow beyond cathectic attachment into a genuine capacity to love, and include more and more "others" from the "they" world.

Our kinship circle, starting with whomever we define as "family" (this can be based on blood ties or any other commonalities defining a group we identify with as "mine") mirror for us who we are to be and what we are to believe, and convey the negative consequences of not meeting their behavioral expectations.

This is often not explicit, but we absorb it in subtle and initially non-verbal ways. For good or ill, family always shapes us and restricts us even as it nurtures and protects us. Its norms are always to some degree procrustean, depending on how much of our nature needs to be "cut off" to fit the acceptable mold. If we were born with natural inclinations or interests beyond acceptable familial limits, our individuality and, if we let it, the unique life we were born for may be derailed or even aborted. Paradoxically, this may be a greater danger with really "good" parents whom we want desperately to please, so this is one case where good parents can be subtly more "subversive" than bad ones. "Bad" parents can be easier to defy and leave.

The Emotional/Kinship Center gives us our name and molds our life, setting basic lifelong habit patterns. It is here that we learn what our talents and limits are (as seen by our elders); it is also here that our "wings are clipped" to the size our kin consider proper, lest we try to fly higher and farther than the collective vision allows.

I am reminded here of the dream of an 11-year-old boy many years ago which speaks to this. In the dream, he was playing outside his actual home when several friendly boys arrived and invited him to play with them. They told him they could fly, and would teach him, too. He was excited at the prospect, but just at that moment a woman dressed in black arrived and sternly told him he had no business playing with those boys, much less flying. He was to get into the house immediately and stay there. She grabbed his arm to make sure he didn't get away and led him into the house. At this point, his dream ended. He felt sad but resigned.

An interpretation of this dream is not relevant here. We have no way of knowing whether "flying" with the boys would have been better for him at that time than staying in a house on firm ground, even though he didn't like it in the dream. The point here is that this kind of imposed restriction happens to us often, whether from the outside or self-generated. Sometimes it is the sensible thing to do. But how often do we unconsciously place unnecessary limits on our inner development or outer achievements in order to not violate (at least not too much) the suitable family or collective "ceiling" to what is deemed "possible" or "acceptable" – that is, what the kinship circle can tolerate without consigning the deviating member to psychological (or even physical) exile?

Historically, such a process is vividly illustrated by the Amish practice of punishment by "shunning," in which a serious transgression of collective behavioral rules resulted in the whole group refusing thenceforth to acknowledge the presence of the person in any way whatsoever, thereby totally isolating the offender – with devastating psychological and often also stress-induced physical consequences, even death.

Less drastic examples of this that I have heard of, and personally worked with, are people who get stuck at a point in their life where they feel they have gone too far beyond their parents or kinship group members in worldly achievement. Perhaps this also applies to psycho-spiritual development.

Most are not aware of this feeling or why they are stuck. They simply feel uneasy, blocked, unhappy and anxious, which is what sometimes brings them to therapy or some other form of introspective searching.

I have worked with several graduate students, men and women from modest backgrounds where they were the first in their families to finish college and/or work toward advanced degrees, who did not understand why they were unable to finish their theses or dissertations even though they knew they had the ability to do so. In several cases, they even had all their data collected and all that remained was the final writing and analysis, yet they stopped, as if paralyzed.

What emerged from our work together was a strong but unconscious fear of "flying too high" and losing their connection to family and roots in the process. For example, having the title "Doctor" attached to their names just felt too foreign, or too much to live up to. They had internalized the "ceiling" beyond which their inner parent and cultural conditioning told them they could or should not go, so they clipped their own wings. The two that come most strongly to mind did finally accomplish what they set out to do and developed successful careers in their fields. I sometimes wonder what the outcome was for the ones about whom I have no further information.

Though we do have choices about whom to include in our kinship group and which groups we wish to belong to as we mature, it is helpful to stay aware of the fact that we never wholly lose our embeddedness in our original social matrix. As our life journey progresses, however, we can transform how we relate to it, and we never have to stay stuck in a situation that is truly inhospitable to our authentic being.

A benign and life-affirming Kinship Center gifts us with healthy emotional development, reflected in basic emotional security, comfort in our body and its sensuality (maturing in adulthood into healthy sexuality and its loving expression), and adequate relationship skills, as well as a solid sense of our place in the social order and the universe. We feel lovable and able to love, although at this stage it is still a cathectic love: "I love you because you love *me*, because you make *me* feel good, because if I love you, you will do this or that for *me*," and so on. We don't recognize how dependent and conditional our loving is, but this kind of dependent attachment is the first step toward unconditional love, and without it as a foundation, we might never learn to love at all.

Our first sense of our spiritual identity is also provided by the religious traditions and structures within which we grow up. Spirit at this stage is usually personified as an all-powerful parental figure, a "Father" in patriarchal cultures such as our own, who expects us to be "good" and obey His commandments (as interpreted by our culture's religious authorities). "If I do what my church says, or at least try hard, God will reward me, and if I sin I shall be punished," is a basic religious stance. The balance of lovingness vs. punitiveness in the God worshipped varies among different traditions and sects, but what is clear is that we are His children and here to do His Will. He is *our* God and we are *His* favored children.

The one-sidedness of this masculine deity, as seen in institutional forms of Christianity, Judaism, and Islam, leaves a vacuum in the human psyche. If I am a child of the Divine, where is Mother? A child's first instinct when in need of comfort and support is to turn to its mother – we have only to witness the deep devotion so many Catholics feel toward the Virgin Mary even though she is not officially a deity. Unique among these three traditions, however, she has developed into a quasi-divine figure personifying the positive aspects of the ancient Great Goddess or Great Mother: ever compassionate and nurturing, never punitive, ready to comfort us and intervene on our behalf (with the all-powerful male God, in this case).

It has been suggested that the materialism of our time is a form of our longing for the security of the Mother, literally a mater-ialism (mater being the Latin word for mother). Money can provide a lot of creature comforts and security that we would want from the ideal mother, since the sense of belonging to the Earth as a mother who provides us and our kin with basic sustenance and a sense of being part of something bigger than our little selves is largely lost in our technological and largely urban culture.

Still, we need human connection, and like orphan baby monkeys who will cling to fuzzy inanimate objects when no live mother is available, we, too, seek substitutes when the real thing is not available.  Do we cling desperately to our material trophies in hopes of compensating for inadequate human contact and warmth?  Do we use our "transitional objects" in the form of things and power symbols to create the illusion of a spurious security as a way to buffer our fear of becoming "orphans"?  The hopeless futility of such an attempt merely feeds our greed for ever more money, status, and the external power and security we hope they will bring. As the saying goes, we can never have enough of what we don't really want.

This naturally leads to a discussion of Center THREE, but first, here are some questions for you to ponder about the Kinship Center and how it has influenced your life, followed by a few concluding comments:

• Who are you when you are with your family?  How did you learn that role?

• How does it manifest now?  Has it changed, or not? Do you feel you "belong"?

• What imprints of the cultural/familial matrix you were born into do you still carry, such as worldview, values, religious beliefs, rituals, behaviors?

• Which of them fit who you are now? Which sub-personalities from this Center are still active in you? Have they changed? Do they support your wholeness?

• How has this Center shaped your sexuality and self-image as a mate or lover? Do you feel comfortable with your sensuality? Is your body happy?

• What are/have been your major cathectic objects?


All of us grow up through Centers ONE and TWO, however successfully or not. And we never completely leave them, even if we find our home Center somewhere else and no longer share their worldview. The bulk of humanity continues to live here, and wonderful examples of well developed, healthy Survival and Kinship centered cultures exist even now, with a rich cultural legacy and spiritual tradition. Hawaii exemplifies this for me, and the wisdom teachings of the Island elders are still alive in its land and people – even those of us who came from elsewhere and were lucky enough to live there long enough to absorb some of it. I lived in Hawaii for sixteen years, and still think of it lovingly as the land of my spiritual birth.

I have not explicitly discussed sexuality here, although it is associated with the chakra related to Center TWO, which is often called the sexual chakra. It is obviously also associated with Center ONE. Yet sexual energy is interwoven with all other aspects of the seven Centers, and to discuss it adequately is beyond the scope of this book. I offer the following simplified formulations simply as an acknowledgment of the importance of sexual energy as it moves through us at different times and a reminder of its multi-layered complexity, so as not to limit its expression to Center TWO alone.

Sex is a primary human drive – for procreation and physical pleasure at ONE, for pleasure and emotional bonding at TWO, for feelings of potency and/or conquest at THREE. At FOUR, love that extends beyond cathectic attachment becomes more important than sex as such, at FIVE we search for both soul communion and a "soul mate," and SIX seeks a unified experience of bliss that is both sexual and beyond physical sex. I have no basis for comments on sexuality at Center SEVEN, but assume that it integrates all these aspects in a way that is spontaneous and fits each specific situation.

Modern psychology has explored the development of the first two foundational Centers, as well as Center THREE's focused egoic development, quite thoroughly. Countless books are available covering these developmental stages in their many aspects, so I am only reviewing them briefly, in broad strokes, from the perspective of this model. They will become relevant again to our explorations further on when we revisit them as part of our psycho-spiritual journey during the return cycles which get triggered when we move or are thrust by life beyond the "in-law" world.

# CHAPTER THREE

# EGO, POWER, AND MASTERY

*Center THREE: Apotheosis of the Ego*

It is a beautiful summer day – the wind warm enough to be caressing, the sun circumspect enough in its heat to make walking a joy. I sit on a rock by an emerald-colored lake in the Southern Oregon mountains, under an ancient oak that offers just enough shade to ward off sunburn. A perfect spot to meditate, except

> *roaring power boats*
> *cleave a stinky oily wake*
> *no more peaceful lake.*

A solitary sailboat drifts among them, at one with wind and water, bobbing up and down and sideways every time the choppy wake of a passing roar-boat hits it. The forced thrust of heavy horsepower cleaves the peaceful surface of smooth, crystal water, leaving a dirty-looking foamy wake higher than the boat itself and seeding the soft breeze with essence of gasoline. Ego making waves, showing Mother what it can do! Leaving its mark behind. Shattering the silence and peace of this pristine place.

I have the sense of witnessing a rape, with the perpetrators oblivious to what they are leaving behind. They are simply having fun, and take for granted that nature is there for them to use. The feeling of speed and thrust that is part of the experience of power-boating is exhilarating – I have felt it, too. And when they are gone, the water will return to tranquility. Mother will do her best to clean the air again of the pollution they left behind, until next weekend, or sooner.

In approaching Center THREE, the Egoic/Power Center, I am tempted to simply say: "Look at the world around you." As in the story above, here we are. This is our daily life. We deal with Ego and achievement, power and mastery, the goal of "making it in this world." Whether or not it suits us as individuals, this is our cultural center of gravity today. It is the water in which we swim. Whether for good or ill depends on what power is used for, on what we are trying to master, on what we define as achievement. So far, it looks like a very mixed bag.

Before going further, I would like to differentiate between the meaning of my capitalized use of the word Ego here, which will become quite clear as we go along, and the sense of individuality as a life or mind-stream that we also refer to as *I*. This *I* serves as the center of our agency in the world, as well as the inner experiencer of the Life that is living its story through us.

This latter *I*, incorporating the positive fruits of the first two Centers and the resulting realistic confidence in our capacities and ability to respond appropriately to both good and bad experiences, is essential to our wholeness as human beings. It will stay with us throughout our human journey, even when we no longer identify with it in the same way we do now. Ego, on the other hand, thinks of itself as a separate, sovereign agent of its own will, king of its own domain, with the assumption that it can and should set its own terms and control its own destiny.

As we move to the Egoic Center developmentally, we expand our horizons into the wider world, where we aspire to "make our mark," "do our own thing," "play our role," or however else we might express it. Our goal becomes whatever our culture defines as success through the development of those intellectual, social, and practical skills needed to achieve it. Both what constitutes "success" and what skills are collectively most valued tend to vary according to the predominant home Center of a given culture, its social structures and stratification, and the acceptable gender roles and norms it endorses.

The social skills mastered through kinship and cultural conditioning are now used largely to serve the purposes of Ego. It is important to note that Ego in this sense refers not only to the solitary, separate self as we think of it in our individualistic culture and as defined above, but can functionally also be a collective Ego, based on personal, cathectic identification with members of our family, clan, nationality, religion, lineage, etc. This is the collective *We* carried over from Second Center kinship structures, and we consider this *We* superior to and different from an alien *They* that includes everybody else. I have come to think of the defensive stance automatically elicited by any actual or perceived criticism or attack against this extended Ego circle as *Fortress We*. When feeling a threat, we pull up the drawbridge and man the barricades.

In healthy development, individual and collective, these cathectic identifications are substantially retained, but adapted to changing circumstances, such as when the culture itself moves toward the values and structures of Center THREE rather than TWO. This brings some softening of *Fortress We* defensiveness while retaining its function as container and protector of valued traditional values and customs. Japan could be seen as a prime contemporary example of such a process, and some other Asian nations seem to be following suit.

We now learn to compete and measure our success by a win/lose balance sheet based on the reward systems of our social environment. This competitive quest to "win" at all cost becomes the prime goal of Ego in all its manifestations: a "phallic thrust" that seeks self-perpetuation in symbolic and material form. Control is important to us now, over others and/or ourselves, and we strive to mobilize worldly power to create what *our* mind envisions.

Where earlier we tried to control significant others to get our needs (and wants) met, we now want to control as much of our environment and material world as possible. Since we can only do so much as individuals, we also try to enlist other people to support *our* goals and aspirations. Most of our healthier aspirations now involve success in some form of rewarded and respected work in the world, allowing us to feel special in some way. On the other hand, in a negative vein, we can also become power-hungry "control freaks" who use others in the service of personal self-aggrandizement.

Developing the confidence and self-mastery necessary to be effective in this pursuit is part of the process. We seek a feeling of self-esteem and competence through the mastery of skills that we value, sometimes based on what our society values, and sometimes more independently determined, in which case we may end up pushing the envelope of social adjustment and collective approval. If the two coincide, we have smooth sailing; if they do not, we may be on a collision course with conventional norms.

This can go in several directions. We can become "outlaws" in the sense described earlier, seeking a broader context while adapting to the realities of the status quo, or we can become rebels of a constructive or destructive kind – an example of the former being the men and women who created the country and the constitutional republic we live in. The latter we know all too well.

In addition to the United States, Western civilization as a whole, with both its flaws and achievements, reflects the multiple faces of Center THREE. It is not surprising, then, that most schools of psychology and most of our psychological research deal with Center THREE functioning both in its healthy and unhealthy aspects. The positive fruits of healthy development through this Center are the qualities of adult competence, responsibility, appropriate relatedness, and self-esteem. Also, what we call "guts." This is a trait much admired in Americans by other peoples: our "can do" attitude, our willingness to set a novel course and make it work, our individualistic self-confidence (which can easily slide into arrogance). These are valuable and even heroic traits when used in the service of positive ideals. This is also essentially modern psychology's consensual definition of a well-adjusted or healthy personality.

When asked for his definition of the healthy adult, Freud gave a very simple answer: "*lieben und arbeiten*" (the ability to love and to work), which pretty much sums it up. Without this, further growth is not possible. Because of this, healthy development of Center THREE matures into the adult functioning required for further development as a whole human being. What is missed here will leave a weak link in our personality and form trailers, eventually leading to the need for "return work," which we will address at length in the chapters that follow.

On the negative side, the competitive and self-enhancing energy of this Center can also move toward excessive self-centeredness and become arrogant, egotistical, grandiose, and intolerant of anything or anybody that threatens personal power or persona. We then want to see ourselves as superior, and whoever is different or disagrees with us as necessarily inferior.

A competitive view of the world – being "better than"

others in all the ways that Ego thinks count – is the prevailing perspective of this stance. That is why I see this developmental phase, which seems to be sweeping the globe at this point in history, as an "apotheosis of the Ego," taking the form of different and competing *Fortresses I* and *We* on a collision course, with little apparent appreciation of the interdependence that sustains us all on this planet. It is a short step from competition to conflict and from conflict to war and oppression, unless some more important value countervails.

The narrowing of our collective vision which results from this kind of Egoic power-bound myopia is potentially devastating to our collective psychological and spiritual development, and ultimately to the future of humanity and our fragile planet. Movement to a larger and ultimately transpersonal view of ourselves is crucial to our survival through the 21st century. What this means developmentally is that there has to be a critical mass of people with sufficiently developed Aloha consciousness (emerging next at Center FOUR) to stop our collective stampede into a blind alley in time. The good news is that there do seem to be more and more people who, having obtained the accoutrements of success that their culture told them would make them happy, find a growing emptiness inside and are looking for "something more" to fill that emptiness.

The bad news is that there are others, emerging from the strictures of rigid kinship tradition, who seem intoxicated with the perceived freedom of a more individualistic, power-based lifestyle. Their idea of "something more" is still tied up with power, prestige, and possessions. More likely to be the young and those marginalized by the traditional systems, they are racing giddily into the modern consumerist world. In the less industrialized countries, the young are doing so with no idea that the benefits of such "progress" bear a price in alienation and disruption of stable social systems. For better and for worse, these systems have provided them with a circumscribed but dependable and comforting source of identity, as well as clear rules of behavior. Acquiring a lot of freedom without sufficient breadth of psycho-spiritual development to use it wisely can be a recipe for personal and social disaster.

We see a lot of polarization and strife in these societies, because the race toward the new in some generates a reactionary wave in response from others who fear change and are invested in tradition. In periods of rapid change and increasing openness to diverse ways of being and believing, we also see an increase in fundamentalism and a reactionary re-consolidation of the worst forms of Kinship Center chauvinism, not to mention Center ONE survivalist repression to protect against perceived threats to familiar, cathected territory.

Such polarization tends to drown out the voices of those who see the need for an evolutionary rather than revolutionary approach: to keep what works well from the past, and at the same time modify that which needs to adapt to present and projected future circumstances. As always in such volatile situations, the fires of passion tend to wipe out the calm solidity of humane reason. As mentioned earlier, the tragedy of 9/11 seems to have precipitated such regressive and polarizing reactions in our own country, especially in our political leadership.

It is interesting that we were hit symbolically at all of the three Centers we have discussed so far: our commercial economy (THREE) as symbolized by the World Trade Center; collectively as Americans who felt a kinship with the victims (TWO); and our survival fears (ONE)—no one is truly safe, so we can't trust anyone any more. The ultimate consequences of our contraction as a nation into a *Fortress*

*We* mentality remain to be seen, but fear and power-driven policies and politics, in their very nature, do not augur well for our remaining models of human progress for the rest of the world.

On the hopeful side once more, the humanistic vanguard and, more recently, an increased interest in spirituality and its inclusion in more integral developmental theories and models, are pointing toward the possibility that our cultural center of gravity may be shifting toward a more spacious worldview. And as saints, sages, shamans and visionaries of all traditions have done through the ages, there are also those among us who are scouting ever further into the unexplored possibilities of an emerging future.

Yet with materialism and material progress as the predominant values (some have called this our secular religion), atheism and/or an indifference altogether to issues of larger meaning and purpose in our lives are common stances of an Ego that thinks itself in charge of its world. This is a comforting view for Ego because it renders irrelevant any "higher power" beyond itself.

Contemporary science also remains caught in materialism, limiting its scope to what it can objectively measure by technical means. Because of its great technical achievements and the respect accorded to science and scientists, a social/ philosophical/ cultural superstructure has arisen that devalues or disregards anything outside its defined scope. This limits officially valid ways knowing, and thereby imprisons us in the "in-law" world of the first three Centers, with a touch of compassion and kindness from Center FOUR when Ego feels secure enough to reach out a little.

As with any one-sided approach, its opposite is constellated in response, and we see this polarity emerge as a cross-traditional religious resurgence in its most dogmatic, fundamentalistic forms, both in individuals and social groups. This is not surprising, for these are the forms most compatible with the *Fortress We* lens through which most people see their world. Those of us who have prayed for a broad spiritual awakening on this planet have felt distress at the rise of fundamentalism all around us, which is not what we had in mind. But what did we expect? A form of spiritual expression for deep-water fish that embraces the world beyond water?

Given all this, we tend to relate to Spirit at this Center either not at all (as agnostics or atheists), or through continuing to identify with the divine personifications of Center TWO, who now seem to look and think a whole lot like us. We are convinced that *our* divine image is the right one, and that *our* interpretation of our religion's scripture is *the* correct interpretation. We are seeing God as a reflected Ego image.

If we see our conscious values and desires as the "right" ones, and our particular forms of "progress" (such as economic prosperity, rigid righteousness, technological and intellectual prowess, etc.) as a sure sign of superiority, it is reasonable within this mindset to assume that our values and aspirations are supported by God (however defined). It is a slippery slope from this to justifying devastating wars in which both sides are convinced that "God is with *us*." It even becomes possible to convince ourselves that to kill (in violation of a universal spiritual prohibition shared by all traditions) is a service to our God and will be divinely rewarded.

Thus do even those of us who are sincere in our religious practice fail to integrate the teachings that we have committed to live by and espouse on the Sabbath into our daily lives the rest of the week. Instead, we filter these through whatever kinship allegiances and territorial attachments from Centers TWO and ONE remain important to us. Self-righteousness, image, and self-importance take center stage. We relate to the Divine as an Ego projection rather than something truly transcendent and beyond our small minds to grasp. We manipulate this projection to serve our self-aggrandizement projects, whether that "self" is experienced as individual or collective.

Even the late 20th century human potential movement, with its expressed humanistic and transpersonal value base, was and is not immune to "spiritual materialism," a term coined by the late Tibetan master Chogyam Trungpa to describe Ego's spiritual acquisitiveness. We see so many of us buying into workshops we hope will bring transformation over a weekend, or tasting everything in the spiritual marketplace in the hope of finding the magic pill of overnight enlightenment. The only difference is that now the "better than" competition has to do with who is more "evolved," more "self-actualized," more "spiritual," more "enlightened," etc.

In any case, whatever the playing field of the race to succeed, in the "race to grace" (as my spiritual teacher puts it) our disowned parts and trailers get short shrift. In its race to be a "winner" and not a "loser," Ego tries to disown these, dismissing them as non-existent or something "I have dealt with." This can be particularly insidious when it is a partial truth used in the service of denial, thereby creating an obstacle to genuine psycho-spiritual growth much harder to deal with than an honest and consciously met shadow eruption, which at least holds the potential for more realistic and multifaceted self-knowledge, warts and all. And that in turn might lead to a heart opening, into compassion and the realization that we are no different from other human beings. No better – or worse. We are ordinary *and* we are special – and so is everyone else.

This is now the movement toward Center FOUR, which I call the Aloha Center. It is also the first and often quiet invitation to the Aloha Waltz, a return cycle we will explore in some detail in the next chapter. Our response here involves a crucial choice. We can extend our *I/We* identifications, our care and concern, to more and more people outside our kinship groups and Ego-enhancement circles, accepting them as equals with the same wants and needs as we have. Or we can shrink back into our old patterns and do more and more of what didn't make us happy before, as a frightened Ego fleeing at the prospect of its threatened demise.

Because we don't distinguish between the separate, fixed, *Me/Mine* Ego, and the contextual *I* that designates a flowing, individual mind-stream interdependently connected with all of existence, we identify with the former and fear total annihilation should that Ego dissolve into the flowing lifestream of the interdependent *I*. The choice to open to this timeless flow will expand our consciousness and further our maturation both psychologically and spiritually, while the choice to contract back into old forms, which may feel like a comfortable alternative to the risk and uncertainty of change, will keep us stuck and stagnant.

Staying within the known mindscape and familiar structures of the "in-law" world will keep Ego intact, even if it proves unsatisfactory in deeper ways. Transformative change, such as an actual shift of our "home base" to the next Center, bringing with it a radical shift in worldview and scope of awareness, is by its very nature disorienting and can feel like a loss and an intimidating encounter with the unknown. For proud Ego, it brings dethronement if not yet death. Small wonder that opting for the status quo or even regression, and *not* in the service of transcendence in this case, appeals to a lot of us at this point.

For example, a policeman once consulted me because he was being told by his superiors that he was falling down on the job by being "too soft" with teenagers brought in for drug offenses. He himself as a teenager had briefly sought in drugs refuge from a conflict-laden and sometimes violent home situation, and so he tried to empathize rather than criticize, often being able to persuade the kids to accept psychological help.

He told me that one of his own youthful experiences with LSD had taken him into "cosmic space" where he felt totally at one with all creation, experiencing it as full of love. His ordinary self disappeared altogether, which frightened him. He thought he was going crazy, and the peaceful, loving space of oneness changed into a nightmarish effort to escape. Fortunately, he sought help at a drug clinic, and was lucky in finding a skilled counselor who helped him realize that his experience was what contemplative religious traditions call a "unitive experience."

His recognizing this as a valuable glimpse into a transpersonal reality led to a more compassionate way of treating people when he went into police work as an adult, but this was misinterpreted by his superiors and led him to wonder whether he really was fit to be a cop. He came to realize that his way of being "soft" was actually a strength and a gift to those who were able to respond to it. I wonder if that would have been the outcome had he not been open enough to seek therapy, even though all he needed was someone to reflect back to him what he already knew but was led to doubt by those with a different and more conventional worldview.

I have used the term "transpersonal" several times now, and this seems an appropriate place to clarify what I mean by that before I talk about it further, especially since the authentically transpersonal is, for Ego, always associated with the unknown, and because of its drive to "know," Ego always tries to explain the transpersonal in terms of something known. Literally, transpersonal means "beyond the personal," but it is not analogous to "collective," which is beyond the personal only in the sense that it refers to group rather than individual phenomena, and frequently manifests merely as an extended *We-Ego*.

Transpersonal, in this context, points to those values, ideas, and sources of knowledge and behavior which are beyond our personal Egoic and Kinship Center identifications, beyond our personal we/they and either/or mindsets.  For example, *my* consciousness is personal; consciousness as such is transpersonal. This model moves from the personal to the transpersonal.  The post-Egoic Centers beyond FOUR are transpersonal when inhabited as a home center or temporarily "visited" as a "preview of coming attractions," but personal when their energies serve to support one of the three foundational Centers.

We all have transpersonal experiences from time to time.  Some of us recognize them as such, some don't, as the policeman in the above story at first did not.  If recognized, they can serve as beacons on our way to full awakening.  However, if they become something Ego identifies with, these "previews of coming attractions" from a Center we are not yet ready to inhabit can become real obstacles.  It is easy for Ego to co-opt even genuine psychological and spiritual breakthroughs to polish its own image.  A "special little me" gremlin is sitting here on my shoulder even as I write this, and I have to be mindful of its illusion that *it* is doing the writing, or that the results are of any momentous significance.  I mention this only as a call for you, too, to notice this Egoic presence ever lurking in the shadows, waiting for an opportunity to reclaim its throne.

A spiritual or psychological epiphany that is followed by a zealous campaign to induce others to join us in our new way of thinking reflects such an Ego intrusion, as do all forms of fervent missionary zeal.  This is one common example of what I am cautioning against, especially after psycho-spiritual breakthroughs.  It is traditional in Buddhism that teachers only teach when asked (and sometimes have to be asked three times, to make sure it is a serious request). In addition, all kinds of proselytizing are discouraged for teachers and students alike. That makes a lot of sense to me in the context of this discussion.

No matter how much we have worked with our shadowy gremlins, we have to be aware that waves of Ego and shadow arisings are a part of our human drama, and part of our psycho-spiritual growth process is learning to ride them out without identifying with them. We know that waves come and waves go, yet our essence, like the ocean, remains unchanged by the surface turbulence.

The perennial human search for "more" and "deeper" is, at its core, driven by our spiritual essence (in the Buddhist tradition, our Buddha nature), which is our true nature. We might think of it as a sort of spiritual homing instinct. Somewhere inside us we feel connected to the greater stream of life that flows through us, but as long as we are confined to identifying with only the *Me and Mine* – or the collectively extended Ego of *Us and Ours* – we remain separate and psychologically encapsulated.

In a broader context, we are seeing such an encapsulation process in our own country today in the oversimplified identification of ourselves as American, as an *Us* against a *They* out to get us, or more locally, as "red states" and "blue states." Is this supposed to describe this incredibly diverse nation? Even in cases where we have come to feel a broader kinship with those different from us, as long as we are not awake to the true nature of our inner drive toward "more" and "deeper," it works through Ego and is easily co-opted by Ego, even in its positive forms. We see this, too, in our broader social tapestry, as in well-intentioned social action that sometimes becomes rigid, strident, and even violent.

It is interesting that the Ego itself plays a crucial role in our movement between Center THREE and Center FOUR. Without its raw energy in quest of "more," we might have never embarked on a psycho-spiritual journey in the first place, nor arrived where we are now. This gives credence to the well-known axiom in transpersonal psychology that we have to be somebody before we can be nobody – that is, we have to have a strong-enough Ego to be capable of consciously putting itself in the service of something greater than itself.

Though it doesn't mean we have to be a big success, a big "somebody" in the outer world, it helps to have experienced enough hunger for "more" and enough experiences of "mores" that did not quench our thirst to realize that we have to look elsewhere for what we really seek. The search is still for personal gratification, but the span of the search has widened, both inwardly and outwardly, and may now begin to expand toward transpersonal realms.

The time of life we get to this point – if we ever do – varies greatly, which is perhaps why the "midlife crisis" has been placed anywhere from our thirties through our fifties. Some of us seem to be born with a capacity to see the limits of Ego gratification sooner than others, or to learn our lessons through fewer disappointments. Being a fast learner may well bring us trans-Egoic experiences sooner, but it does not necessarily shorten the path itself. Nor does it necessarily make spiritual (or, for that matter, psychological) development easier. What it may in fact do is make the obstacles more subtle, and leave openings for Ego to return to power that are more devious and therefore harder to notice. So a facility for transcendence of this kind can be a mixed blessing if we have not solidly developed our foundational centers ONE, TWO, and THREE in a healthy way.

Now, some reflection questions for you on your experience of Center THREE:

- In which areas of your life do you feel powerful? Successful? Competent?

- How does that manifest behaviorally? How do you deal with your insecurities and /or what you deem "failures"?

- How do you exercise power and authority? Do you enjoy doing so? If so, why? If not, why?

- Would you like to be famous? If so, for what? If not, is there something you would like to be admired for?

- If you unexpectedly received a large monetary windfall of far more than you need to cover your living expenses, how would you use the surplus? How would your life be different? How might it change you? What specific temptations might arise?

- What do you consider your greatest life achievement so far? Why?

# CHAPTER FOUR

# AN INVITATION OF THE HEART

## Center FOUR: The Aloha Waltz

The day will come when we shall harness for
God the energies of love.  And, on that day, for
the second time in the history of the world, the
human being will have discovered fire.

Teilhard de Chardin

There comes a time when more is not enough – more money, more applause, more success, more popularity, more possessions.  A subtle, growing, insistent feeling may then come upon us that feels like homesickness for a place or a something we do not know but have a deep, vague feeling will finally make us happy.  In our culture, this diffuse longing may develop into a mid-life crisis, except that it can just as well happen sooner or later, depending on when we reach this developmental juncture.

What we are sensing here is an invitation from the depths of us to an inner dance I call the "Aloha Waltz."  My use of "Aloha" here rather than "Love" comes from my feeling that love is one of the most misused words in our language, designating everything from addictive possessiveness to simple preference, to romantic intoxication, up to and including unconditional caring and divine compassion.  Aloha, in its original sacred meaning, is clearer.

According to the late Hawaiian Elder Nana Veary, in *Change We Must: My Spiritual Journey,* "*Alo* means the bosom, the [heart] center of the universe. '*Ha'* is the breath of God. The word is imbued with a great deal of power. I do not use the word casually. Aloha is a feeling, a recognition of the divine. It is not just a word or a greeting. When you say 'aloha' to someone, you are conveying or bestowing this feeling."

She says that in ancient Hawaii, this honoring of each other as Spirit had no name because it was such an integral part of the culture that it needed none. As times changed and people had to be taught this formerly natural quality, it came to be called "Aloha Spirit." Though diluted by materialism and contemporary American culture, it still lives on in the Hawaii I love.

Nana Veary also says that unconditional love is "more than a sentiment. It is a deep sense of the goodness and the generosity of life. This love is the very essence of life, the creative principle behind everything – spiritually, emotionally, mentally, and physically – ever renewing, revitalizing, bringing joy, harmony, and blessings to everything and everyone it touches." So I think of Aloha as the heart energy and expression of Spirit, the breath that breathes us all, the recognition of our common essence beyond me or mine, you or yours, them or theirs.

The spirit of Aloha, as I learned it during my years in Hawaii, encompasses empathy with the pain *and* joy of others; the idea that we are all equal parts of the Creator and therefore to harm another is to harm oneself; extending open-hearted hospitality whether to friend or stranger; stewardship of the earth and sky and sea which sustain our life; and gratitude for all we receive, taking from nature only what we need and saying thank you. We thank the fish that provide us with food, the flowers for their beauty, and the birds for reminding us of our own capacity to soar.

Aloha is similar to what Buddhists call *bodhicitta* and the early Christians called *caritas*, and this quality forms the core of every authentic spiritual tradition. This is what Center FOUR opens us up to – if not yet as a realization, then as an aspiration, a practice, and a more inclusive attitude. FOUR is a complex Center, both transitional and terminal, because as we move into Center SEVEN, we become permanently rooted in total and unconditional Aloha.

Our popular view of love is most closely identified with passion and/or romantic intoxication, which are intense, exciting experiences we all want to have in our lives. But this focus also confuses us about love, and can lead to the notion that love always brings ecstasy and/or pain, and that if it is not exciting in that way it is not real love. Gut-wrenching "love," however, is a contradiction in terms. Gut-wrenching attraction, lust, cathectic attachment, needy dependency, yes. But real love does not give us a bellyache. It makes us more spacious and joyful, and our belly softens as our heart expands. Think of how holding a cooing, smiling baby makes us feel. Or just sitting with a special someone and watching the sun set.

The transition from THREE to FOUR is a difficult one, because Ego will obviously resist what it perceives as its imminent dethronement. If I am a powerful, solitary, separate being in charge of my life and everything else I can control around me, I am not going to let go of that control for the sake of something or someone who may then control me. Even if we begin to stretch our self-identification beyond the purely personal and to feel a part of something bigger than our small selves, we still identify with this encapsulated, sovereign self and insist on protecting and controlling its designated territory within the world we know.

We can also fool ourselves about the degree of Ego

involvement in the good we do in the name of love. A successful executive who was active in progressive political and social movements once asked me whether I thought he "still had an ego." I didn't know how to respond, because to me he virtually personified Egoic pride and self-righteousness, yet was at the same time idealistic in his thinking and put a lot of energy into furthering the causes he espoused. I just said yes, I thought he did "still have an ego," but also affirmed the ideals he tried to implement in the world. He deserved credit for his good intentions, even if his effectiveness in implementing them was compromised because others could see in him what he himself could not.

This man illustrates the trap of espousing Aloha ideals without having done some serious inner work and grappled with our shadow side. The self-righteous arrogance of the resulting belief that we know the right way, including what is right for others, often carried to the point of forcing our ideals upon others, undermines the possibility of authentic growth into genuine Aloha. We cannot achieve Aloha-based ideals through power-based means, any more than we can bomb a totalitarian regime into freedom and democracy. Or preach anybody into "bettering" themselves – unless the willingness is already present. This form of espousing Center FOUR ideals is self-defeating and potentially harmful.

It takes genuine grounding in Aloha to generate more Aloha in the world. That holds true whether we are talking about individuals, groups, nations, or whole civilizations. Very few leaders in our world have understood this – Gandhi, Desmond Tutu, Martin Luther King, Mother Teresa, and the still living and universally respected Dalai Lama come to mind, but the list is short.

A real shift of our psycho-spiritual home base to Center FOUR is of momentous importance, even in its initial tentative phases, and even if we still revert to old Egoic patterns much of the time. At least we are now aware that we are doing so. The Ego loosening required to open to Aloha is progressive, going through many layers of experience (and struggle) before we can make a definitive transition, and even then Ego remains active in the background, making frequent "cameo appearances" when the opportunity arises.

Perhaps the one quality that most consistently demonstrates true Aloha is unfailing kindness toward everyone regardless of who they are. This is also the quality the Dalai Lama has emphasized more than any other in all his writings and public talks, and Mother Teresa lived it in the most challenging conditions imaginable.

### From Love of Power to the Power of Love

How does a genuine shift of this kind happen? The capacity for Aloha grows through the first of the return cycles which I call the Aloha Waltz, danced with conscious attention. At first, these two vital energies strive to dance in harmony while both are trying to lead. The outcome of this struggle will determine whether we remain basically centered in Ego's need for primacy at Center THREE and continue to use the energies of the heart center mostly for self-enhancement in the world (though also for good works as a helpful by-product). Or we may slide back to Center TWO and possibly mistake a renewed or new cathectic attachment for growing Aloha. Hopefully, Ego will voluntarily yield its primacy and use its considerable intellectual and practical skills as a willing partner in compassionately serving the purposes of Aloha in the world.

Being a complex and multi-layered Center, the first layers of Aloha are not yet spiritual as such. If all goes well, however, our identity begins to stretch beyond the purely personal. By personal I also mean Egoic identification with groups based on we/they perception, even if they espouse transpersonal ideals, such as peace. We begin to feel a part of something bigger than our individual selves, however we conceive of that.

The layers of this abundant Center deepen as we develop toward wholeness across all the Centers, but Aloha is likely to first manifest through the birth of trans-cathectic compassion that goes beyond cathectic attachments, including an enhanced sense of community and an impulse toward service that does not arise from kinship values or narcissistic needs alone. Personal power and self-enhancement are no longer primary, at least much of the time.

We also develop our ability to compassionately witness our own behavior and inner process, as well as that of others. For the first time, we can consciously see what Ego is doing and gently de-condition unhelpful habit patterns we didn't recognize before. We can also appreciate the achievements and skills we have mastered which can now serve the values we are newly committed to. While we were wholly identified with Ego, we did not have much capacity for this kind of witnessing.

Having acquired confidence in our place in the world and ability to take care of ourselves, we are now more able to be generous with others as well. A basic cognitive shift occurs from seeing the world in terms of either/or to seeing it as both/and. Forgiveness becomes easier. We can extend our circle of care in ever-widening circles – to our fellow humans and ultimately to all other living beings, including Mother Earth. This span of consciousness is humane, inclusive, and caring, but not yet transpersonal because it functions within the worldview of the in-law world, though expanding its boundaries somewhat.

For some of us, this will suffice to provide a fulfilling life, as we join those caring, socially engaged people who form the backbone of community service all over the world. For others, this may extend further, to a feeling of kinship with all people and/or all of life, so that we/they perception yields to the "we" of our common humanity and even beyond, to all forms of life.

If we have lost, denied, or rejected a divinity of our earlier years, we may discover a renewed connection to spirituality, perhaps in a different form. At this stage, we tend to experience the ultimate Ground of Being we all share in less parental and/or judgmental forms than earlier. Rather, we experience the Divine more as a loving Being, or simply Love without a need to personify it, and we express this in the world in the form of empathy and compassion, the impulse to help ease suffering and promote happiness wherever we can.

When we consider the total human family, few actually get to this stage in a conscious way. Even fewer actually negotiate the full transition from the love of power to the power of Love (that is, a well-developed Aloha Center as their home base). Such a transition is a monumental milestone in our psycho-spiritual development.

We are now at the threshold of a trans-Egoic worldview. Most often, this is our first recognition and aspiration in that direction, a peek through the gate at the garden of Aloha and beyond – a fish jumping briefly out of the water and realizing that water is only part of a whole world to be explored. But that world is still unknown.

What does happen is that we open to a whole new possibility in recognizing that there are limits to our ability to control not just others but ourselves, and that what lies beyond the separate self is so much bigger than our precious *I and Mine.* So there is now an aspiration toward personal and often also spiritual growth which does not primarily seek to enhance our personality but seeks to develop Aloha. We want to move toward wisdom and love of our fellow beings; we aspire to goodness and the capacity for unconditional love. We want happiness more than self-righteousness.

Except in the very rare cases of sudden enlightenment, this is still basically grounded in Ego's wish for the *I* to become better, so it can more accurately be seen as an aspirational entry into the Aloha center, encompassing more than a Center THREE value system. It is humanistic, including most if not all of humanity in our circle of care and wanting all to have the opportunity to grow and to prosper, but it is not yet transpersonal. That will require Ego's abdication of its throne, as it puts itself in the service of a greater, more spacious, transpersonal Self, perhaps at first experimentally and conditionally, before undergoing a complete transformation.

So where is the "gate" from personal to transpersonal? Though I used the term "transpersonal gate" in an article I wrote ten years ago, I do not use it any longer because it implies a sudden shift – now you are on this side and now on that. As noted above, such a sudden shift in our perception of ourselves and of reality can happen, but when it does it has nothing to do with walking through a passage from a "here" to a "there." I now see it as more accurate to think in terms of first excursions from in-law reality. When our minds stretch toward something more encompassing and inclusive than we have known before, we make short visits to a trans-Egoic reality. This can evolve into longer and more frequent "vacations," until we finally feel at home.

It is likely, probably somewhere in the liminal interface of the Star Center (FIVE) and finding ourselves drawn into the Sophia Task (Center SIX), that our view of ourselves and reality *will* undergo a radical change, and will become irreversibly transpersonal. It may well feel like a surprise: like the butterfly which, if you stop chasing it, comes and sits gently on your shoulder and you suddenly notice it is there. No bells and whistles. Quite ordinary, and completely natural as far as the transpersonal Self is concerned. But how extraordinary on the personal level when it happens! And however unlikely, it *can* happen *now*.

A fully actualized FOUR is about living Aloha, and seeing our own ultimate essence in everyone and everything. Opposites can now be held in harmony, giving each its due even if they cannot be rationally reconciled at the moment. We can respect each other's beliefs and spiritual traditions even if they differ from our own. Imagine our world and its social institutions if this attitude became the foundation of our social and political actions. According to reports of those attending, a recent council of world religious leaders of different traditions was imbued with this feeling, and the delegates came home newly inspired and hopeful that world peace and understanding across formal differences are really possible, if only a sufficient number of us walk far enough down our spiritual paths.

Having substantially actualized FOUR, we may not necessarily fit the conventional warm and fuzzy image of "nice." In fact, we may be quite tough in our compassion because we understand that being indiscriminately affirming and helpful may not always serve another's deeper growth needs. This is reflected in what we have come to call "tough love." What is true, though, is that we will respect the essence of the other person while responding as appropriately as we can to the situation at hand. Because we cannot always discern from an external action the motivation behind it, or its wisdom or folly in a larger context, it is difficult to distinguish instrumental (i.e. Ego-serving) aloha from genuine Aloha, and so it is best to be careful about the judgments we make

– in either direction. Better yet not to judge at all, and simply appreciate whatever good is being done.

While Center FOUR can bring about a transition from in-law to out-law consciousness, it can also develop to a substantial degree within an in-law reality, as described above. The fish sees light filtered from above as it ventures upriver, and senses something up there, but has not yet recognized it as more than just another aspect of its familiar universe. Water is still not recognized as "water," although our world now seems a little brighter.

I call this the "humanistic bulge," where the conventional in-law paradigm is stretched but not transcended. The humanistic bulge is still Ego-based, except that we now identify with a broader range of people, and the "we" extends to more of humanity – to a greater or lesser degree, depending on how secure we ourselves feel.

This was pretty much the direction I saw us as a nation going before 9/11. Then, this Egoic country with a strong humanistic bent was swept by shock and Survival-based fear into a quick *We-Ego* retaliation against an overly generalized and presumptively culpable "they." What if some measure of Aloha had entered into the initial deliberations leading to our response? What if we had included some thoughtful members of "they" in trying to understand the deeper roots of what happened, and what a strong *and* just response might have been in the light of its effect not just on us but the whole world community?

On a more personal level, we may regress to TWO to avoid the Ego challenges inherent in the felt invitation to FOUR. How many of us, feeling the vague inner call to something deeper and greater, have unconsciously sought in the familiarity of a new personal love relationship the connection with a transpersonal Love, sometimes betraying commitments and breaking up families in the process?

Or tried a new activity, or a new adrenalin rush, or more and more of what didn't satisfy in the first place, be it cars, clothes, big houses, food, travel or anything else, in order to bypass the need to walk into unknown inner territory and meet parts of ourselves we have tried to disown or which we have never had a chance to meet in the first place? What dark and threatening unknowns may lurk in the basement of our consciousness? Better stick with what we know. Our familiar rut may not satisfy, but it is, well – familiar.

Confronting these unknown "gremlins" that go bump in the night of our unconsciousness is humbling. It takes courage. And there is no way around it if we are to become whole. Whether we do it through psychotherapy, other forms of serious inner work, or commitment to an authentic spiritual practice (hopefully under the guidance of a qualified teacher or spiritual guide), do it we must – or stagnate. It was C.G.Jung who said that those who fail to develop psychologically, especially in the second half of life, risk becoming caricatures of themselves as they age. A harsh warning, but worth heeding.

There are many failed THREE to FOUR passages, where habit and entropy triumph over the pull toward wholeness. For many of us, where we are is comfortable enough, so there is little motivation to dismantle the life we have created and know how to manage in order to undertake an unknown journey toward an unknown though perhaps briefly glimpsed destination. Even if glimpsed, do we know it is *really* real? If real, is it worth it? Ego can offer countless reasonable questions and objections against setting sail for this "New World."

Much of what we decry as deterioration in today's industrialized, technocratic societies is the result of a widespread flight from Aloha development. Ego wants to retain its kingship or, in a "developing" society, seek to catch up with the "developed" countries' material abundance, to finally claim its personal crown. The result is a tragic individual and collective narcissism, and its fallout in brutal competition. This is also reflected in a decline of civility and ethics, win-at-all-cost attitudes, violence, suicide, hopelessness, and an epidemic of addictions.

It has been said by many, starting with Jung a century ago, that addictions are a misguided search for some kind of spiritual connection, or at least some kind of transcendent experience. But an experience is just an experience, and so we crave more, and still more. Now the mighty Ego merely continues its march in quest of more experiences. Ultimately, what can stop it is spiritual power fueled by love and a broader understanding of what a spiritual journey entails, and ultimately our own willingness to dance with Love and let it lead.

Paradoxically, we need Ego's help to transcend Ego, and we need Aloha to motivate Ego in that direction. However, we can get stuck and obsessive even here. Aloha depends on our ability to accept and let go freely. It is an unimpeded flow. Only when we learn to accept freely and let go without regret can we enter into this flow and feel a part of it. Everything we grasp too tightly becomes rigid, lifeless, and an obstacle. Burnout may be a sign that we have not yet mastered this freedom of both receiving and letting go. Aloha is for us, too, as well as everyone else. We can only give what we have.

It is likely that not only our individual destiny depends on the awakening of Aloha, but also that of our species and our planet. The potential cost of our ignorance and failure to expand our collective consciousness beyond in-law chauvinism gets higher every day. Even where compassion seems to be taking root, Ego finds ever more subtle ways to try to re-instate its primacy, and to keep it in its proper role takes ever more mindfulness on our part. Even a dethroned Ego, or its "heirs" in the form of trailers, can revert to old habits. It is as though there were a bright neon warning sign flashing before our mind's eye at the threshold of Center FOUR:

> **You have reached the point of transition beyond the in-law world you have inhabited thus far. From here on, the road is not straight. Go back and deal with unfinished business at Center THREE. You must dance the Aloha Waltz until Love and Power work out a balance and your Egoic skills follow Love's lead. With your heart open to compassion and kinship with all of life, you will be ready to inhabit Center FOUR.**

## Accepting the Invitation to Waltz

We do not necessarily choose this dance consciously. We are usually swept up in it by the rhythms of our lives, or else we resist and settle into our familiar status quo and pretend we never heard the music. If you have ever danced a fast Viennese waltz, you know that one person must lead and the other follow. If both try to lead at the same time, they trip over each other's feet and can easily end up in a heap on the floor. And if they do not hold on to each other in a balanced way, the centrifugal force of spinning around may break their connection and throw both off balance. Synchronization and harmony are the requirements of this dance, as they are of a genuine transition from the love of Power to the power of Love. Both qualities are needed, but the quality and richness of our lives depend on whether Love serves Power or Power serves Love.

We may accept the invitation and agree to dance.

Realizing how easily Aloha is contaminated by Ego strivings and power needs, we now accept the necessity to consciously re-visit and deal with our unfinished power issues, lest they corrupt whatever we try to do in the spirit of Aloha. Sincere generosity can easily and imperceptibly slip into self-serving expectations and subtle self-congratulation, and our power drive can so easily co-opt our best inclinations toward compassionate service.

It is all too easy to fall into the trap of the original missionaries who went to Hawaii to do good, but did very well indeed, ending up with most of the land and wealth of the islands. They were probably very sincere in their original intentions to bring their idea of God to people they perceived as godless, but oblivious to the arrogance and self-serving nature of imposing their beliefs on a native culture with rich spiritual traditions of its own.

There are so many failed THREE to FOUR passages, tripped up by Ego attachments or failed courage. The challenges and potholes along this path must not be underestimated. Life itself often arranges some sort of wake-up call in the form of personal trauma or some juicy, humbling experiences to nudge us into this next stage of our journey. If we seek psychotherapy at this point, we usually see our problems as caused by such events. The realization that it was indeed a wake-up call and that we at some level collaborated in bringing it about comes later, and only if we succeed in developing (or already have) some objective self-witnessing capacity.

Most often, several temporarily effective "band-aid" solutions will be tried first, including flight into new jobs, relationships, geographical locations, hobbies, "trying harder" with what doesn't work, and so on, even escaping into spirituality. Therapy is often a last-ditch effort, not infrequently under pressure from a significant other.

Self-help books and workshops are often tried, and they can be helpful, as can a consistent spiritual practice. However, all this may provide only symptomatic relief if the authentic needs of the seedling striving to grow remain unsatisfied.

It is common for us to manifest Aloha energy without our overall consciousness having transitioned to Center FOUR. There is a basic kindness in us that transcends both ego and kinship identifications, and sometimes even our basic survival instinct. This is an expression of our natural heart energy, our deepest nature, and it can express itself through anyone at any stage of overall development – thank goodness. We hear of many spontaneous deeds of heroic self-sacrifice to help or save a perfect stranger, and gestures of generosity and service happen every day.

The response to the 9/11 tragedy, from firefighters and police to ordinary people from all walks of life volunteering help regardless of personal safety considerations, was an extraordinary expression of this basic compassion. So was the worldwide reaction of friendship and support to us as a nation, providing a historic moment when human consciousness could have shifted toward a realization of global kinship. Sadly, that moment passed, and subsequent events seem to have made us more defensive and aggressive than before.

I used to think this passage is easier for women than for men. It seems like a more visible and conscious struggle for more men, who identify more overtly and directly with their Center THREE identity, but it may not actually be easier for women, just more subtle. As women, having been conditioned into Kinship Center roles and social expectations associated with the nurturing qualities of mothering, we are generally less consciously identified with a distinct Ego (in fact, we may never have developed a very strong one). We are more likely to identify with our circle of care and kinship connections, and may not recognize these identifications as Egoic extensions of *Me and Mine*, seeing them instead as FOUR qualities without noticing Ego pulling the strings behind the scenes.

Many worthwhile volunteer activities and civic committees prompted by concern for the greater good, such as PTA's, service clubs like Rotary and Lions, even peace organizations and hospice programs, run into obstacles and spend a lot of time dealing with personality clashes and fixed opinions which relate more to individual agendas than the espoused mission. Competing ego investments can emerge most powerfully in such close associations, and many families are torn apart by lack of conscious resolution of these issues within their own kinship circle.

Even with recent changes, women are called upon more often to do the loving and the nurturing, and therefore we find it easier to empathize and identify with other people. But with whom do we empathize? Whom do we love and nurture? Usually, *our* children, *our* loved ones, *our* kinds of people. What looks like Aloha on the surface needs to be examined more closely, because often it turns out to be just a more broadly extended circle of personal cathexes. What is outside is still "other," and so a mother in one country can grieve over a son or husband killed on her side of a battle and rejoice in the death of another mother's son or husband on the "enemy" side. This is not genuine Aloha.

However laudable and exalted in speech, love is hardly a coin of political exchange. Center THREE leadership may try softer power schemes in the name of diplomacy, but when push comes to shove, what we really believe works is money or force. Force is a method in ONE or TWO societies, money the driver in THREE, and usually the first preference in the

West. First we try to bribe our enemies, then threaten them economically, then threaten force, then use force, then try to bribe them again. Much the same patterns can arise in personal relationships.

Do we then wonder why children in our schools follow in kind, at younger and younger ages? We are seeing bullying and psychological coercion becoming more and more of a problem in our schools, across the whole age spectrum. Are we surprised that our children are emulating what they see in politics, the media, business, and perhaps even in their own homes? If being a "winner," no matter how or at what cost, is our social ideal of success, can we fault our children for picking up the torch we hand them?

However lofty our goals, if the means are not congruent, the outcome will not serve compassion or any other lofty purpose. It will simply increase divisiveness and hatred, even where there was none before, and set the stage for more power clashes later on to even the score, even down the line of generations. Aren't we seeing this happen in our world every day, further amplified by 24/7 media coverage that feeds on conflict and drama?

It is my belief that during this young century and millennium, we are being psychologically and spiritually challenged to expand our consciousness and self-definition to embrace and embody Aloha, not just espouse it as a nice ideal. That applies especially to those of us who have used, and often abused, both the positive and negative powers and achievements of the Egoic realm, and are fidgeting at the edge of a new awakening. What we fear we might wake up to or have to give up in the process holds us back as much as our deeper nature of Aloha struggles to break through and push us forward.

Having come this far, and having at least intellectually accepted the spiritual premise that we are all equal manifestations of Spirit and therefore of one essence, we are now the ones who have to form the "critical mass" that will bring the global Aloha Waltz to the point where Power will finally serve Love. This is now crucial, and has to become an experiential reality held not just in our minds but also in our hearts and our very cells. This reality has to become our home, where we stand without possibility of returning to our separate, Ego-encapsulated selves. This has to guide our actions in the world. If not, we are all in deep trouble, both those who have awakened to that necessity and those who have not. Lack of awareness does not absolve us of its consequences.

Of course, sorting all this out takes fine discernment as well as radical self-honesty, because this discernment can only be done by each one of us for ourselves. Others can act as mirrors and give us feedback on what they see, but they cannot do it for us. Transformation is a do-it-yourself project.

We are now in a liminal space – betwixt and between "here" and "there." We are neither in-laws nor out-laws, and far from being beyond both. We are fish who swim in the water but know it for what it is, and that there is more beyond it. To paraphrase the Book of Genesis, we cannot un-eat the apple. The only viable alternative is to accept the invitation of the unknown and open ourselves to it, one step at a time.

So, as we settle into Center FOUR (if we do), we grow into the ability to compassionately witness our own behavior and inner process, as well as empathize more easily with others. For the first time, we are able to see what Ego is doing and gently de-condition its negative habits. We can also consciously practice generosity toward fellow humans beyond *Fortress I* or *We* while not neglecting our own needs in the process. A basic cognitive shift occurs here, moving from seeing the world in terms of either/or to a both/and view. Divergent views can be held in the spirit of Aloha while each is respected on its own terms. This softening happens slowly but progressively, as we do our part in conscious daily practice of mindfulness and compassion. We have learned to waltz.

While waltzing, we might also contemplate the following questions:

- What/whom do you love without expectations or a personal agenda?

- Who is included/excluded as part of your circle of care?

- Do you see yourself as a compassionate person? A loving person? How do you express this, internally and externally?

- What do you mean when you say "love"?

- What are your Ego's most challenging sabotage maneuvers? How often are you aware of these? How do you deal with them?

- Who are the people you know or have known who, for you, embody Aloha? How have they influenced your life?

# CHAPTER FIVE

# FINDING YOUR OWN TRUE VOICE

## *Center FIVE: The Descent Tango*

The place God calls you to is the place
where your deep gladness
and the world's deep hunger meet.

Friedrich Buechner, *Wishful Thinking*

In looking back at the three foundational Centers, we realize that they were, in contemporary imagery, shopping centers of a sort: for meeting our basic needs, for social status and esteem, for self-satisfaction and comforts and creating a good life. It was where we settled into our world and our place in it. Center FOUR opened us to a broader view of ourselves and our interdependent relationship with others, including all of life. Now we recognize that, deep down, even if our life is going well, we have a longing to "bloom" as the unique expression of Spirit we were meant to be. Whether referred to as "singing my own song," "finding my own voice" or, in Sixties' language, "doing my own thing," it has to do with the sacred meaning of vocation, both on inner and outer levels. We may not think of it in those terms, but we all know the feeling.

I am told some ancient cultures believed that a new star appears in the sky when a child is born, reflecting that new being's unique destiny. It is that child's life task to find and follow that star. James Hillman elaborates on a similar idea in modern terms in his book *Soul Code*, as does Carolyn Gratton in *The Art of Spiritual Guidance*:

> The approach to spiritual direction that is developed in this book accepts a basic assumption about each human person: the human person is a unique, never-to-be-replicated image of the Mystery itself. This way of guidance assumes that each person's life develops as an expression of his or her emerging foundational life form, or embodied soul.
>
> "Spiritual" in this sense refers to who we are, to our distinctively human ability to express this soul personally through our powers of mind and will. . . Spiritual life, then, refers not only to inner life, but is concerned with the entire created field in which that life unfolds.
>
> On the one hand, we have the "call," given to each human person even before birth, to become a unique "diamond." On the other hand, we have the life process of gradually discovering and expressing that call concretely, in dialogue with the changing appeals discovered in the world as it evokes commitments of time and energy in each person throughout life.

This movement toward self-expression that flows from the truth of our Being can be seen as fueled by divine energy. It is not Ego expression, which up to now the energies of this Center were used to serve. The primary qualities of this new level of creativity are that it is not conventional, not competitive, not done for external reasons or rewards. Its goal is to manifest, in our life and in our work in the world, that embodiment of spirit called by our name – in this place where our "deep gladness and the world's deep hunger meet." Except the world is not always aware of such a hunger, or ready to appreciate a particular form of creative expression, especially if new and different. Such has been the experience of many artists and visionaries.

This creativity must be for its own sake, in its own form, out of its own life-stream, and may bring no social or monetary rewards at all. That has been true of many who are now considered cultural icons but were ignored and even reviled during their own lifetime. History shows us that the more fixed in specific forms and beliefs a culture, the more resistant it is to new and non-conforming forms of expression. And the more diversity spreads through such a culture, the more its stability weakens. This can trigger movement within the culture toward both reactionary repression and creative (or destructive) chaos, and produce a lot of emotionality and conflict. Yet the old forms have to break apart in order for new forms to emerge. A middle way here is not easy to find or implement. It is easy to see this in many contemporary societies, including our own, and it also applies to us individually if we are to become whole.

Having established a firm base in Center FOUR, we may now begin to hear an inner call to the Star Center (FIVE). The Aloha Waltz continues, but the focus shifts toward our new direction. Sometimes we know early in life where that is, and sometimes it takes decades or even a lifetime to discover, but the yearning is there nonetheless. This call toward authenticity in self-expression is different from Ego expression, which up to now the energies of Center FIVE were used for. The goal now is to manifest in our life, in some tangible and useful form, the particular gifts of our unique embodiment, as a conscious gift of love and gratitude.

It also involves a shift to a more spacious mental and emotional framework, and arises naturally from the experience and world-view of Aloha rather than being imposed by inner or outer "shoulds." Practical considerations are also somewhat peripheral to this task, though they can help or hinder our progress. Fulfilling a purpose we feel has heart and meaning for us is our contribution to the vast tapestry of Life, and it is important that we weave our unique little thread into its fitting place in the evolving design.

However, before we can know what our little thread looks like and where it belongs, we have major work to do. Before we can walk further on our authentic psycho-spiritual path, we must revisit and integrate aspects of our past, especially trailers of unfinished business – in our relationships, both painful and pleasant, and all the "never was/never will be's" of earlier parts of our life: naming them, mourning them or rejoicing in them, and letting them go.

Some may regret never having had children or not having had the courage to pursue an early passion, others mourn broken marriages or other important relationships – all the wrong roads taken and the roads not taken which wistful fantasy has embellished into alternate realities. This is the time to let go of both rosy fantasies and old grudges, accept that we all do the best we can with the resources and insight we have at any given moment in time, and forgive ourselves and others our errors. Guilt is irrelevant at this point, although an apology and attempt to make amends for a specific harm, if possible, can be very healing.

Whether willingly or under protest, life grabs us and sweeps us into this second return cycle, embroiling us once again in the cathectic patterns and attachments of Center TWO. Because the first two Centers were fused in childhood, this also draws in our physical and survival issues at ONE. I call this FIVE to TWO return cycle the Descent Tango, and it is quite a dance: full of passion, ups and downs, missteps, and inevitable bruises. Ego once more strives to direct the choreography, and it takes discernment based on deep self-knowledge, as well as clarity about what our real values and capacities are, to hold our course. People often enter therapy at this time, especially the forms that are insight and depth-oriented, such as Jungian analysis.

Usually, this is how it begins. We are struggling to do or express in some outward form something that deeply reflects our core values and who we feel we really are. We are not talking about things we simply like, or are temporarily excited about, or that we do mainly for a living, fame, status, or others' approval. On the contrary, this "call of the Seed" may well run counter to these and take us in an unexpected direction, which can be scary because it is new to us and, because we are doing it in our unique way, there are no templates to follow. We create as we go along, directed by an inner impetus that we may have difficulty trusting or understanding, and the outcome is unpredictable. This is so even if we end up outwardly doing pretty much what we have been doing all along – much the same job, same family, same friends – but it will be a different "I" doing it, one viewed with suspicion by Ego and old habit patterns.

We may feel very vulnerable, as though being asked to walk stark naked down Main Street. We want so much to create something worthwhile out of our deep need to manifest our unique gifts, and yet we may feel that we have nothing worth giving, or that what we can give will not be well received. We may fear being criticized or ridiculed, or dismissed as insignificant. Our nightly dreams may reflect these themes.

Since what we are trying to do is unique because nobody has done this *particular* thing in this *particular* way before, all our old inferiority feelings, insecurities, self-criticisms, perceived limitations, fears of humiliation (etc., etc.) are suddenly in our face and stirring in our belly, again. Perhaps we know them all – none of it is new, neither the images nor the sabotaging voices in our head – we just thought we had outgrown them, or hoped we had. Now we have to meet our inner judge and jury again, and stand our ground.

It is essential to realize that this does not mean we have failed and are back where we started. We are simply following a normal growth cycle of revisiting and integrating what was missed before, in the service of our further "blooming."

Whatever the inner-world challenges as we try to crawl from the cocoon of conditioning to become the butterflies we really are, the outer world will supply us with more. Paradoxically, we may find the biggest obstacles and distractions in the people we're closest to: spouse, partner, children, relatives, friends, co-workers. It feels like being caught over and over in an undertow of daily emotional currents pulling us back to old habits, fulfilling old expectations, living up to old norms, so that our Star seems to recede before our eyes with every step we take toward it. This, too, is part of the process. And here, too, we are invited to gently and compassionately hold our ground.

The descent phase of the FIVE - TWO return cycle forces us, for yet another round, into shadow and probably also family-of-origin work. We learn that we really "can't go home again" – and if we discover we can, that may present another problem. The ascent phase from TWO to FIVE challenges us to fight a strong social and emotional undertow as we reach toward our beckoning Star, and this undertow can present itself as love. But it is cathectic love, and it can become a major saboteur of our creative growth. The attachment of the people who love us is to the person they have always known or wanted us to be, and deep down they may be more comfortable with that even if they rationally support the changes we are going through.

We resist change, especially when it seems to threaten us with losing something we have experienced as dependable, and in-law human nature in particular has always valued the known and the familiar. Since the Tango is a very absorbing process that requires a lot of deep self-witnessing, as well as periods of silence and solitary inner work, this inwardness may be experienced by others as rejection.

They may feel distanced by our lowered cathectic invest-ment in familiar behavior patterns (theirs as well as ours). They may be puzzled or uncomfortable with interactions that do not conform to habitual patterns. They may feel discounted, and perceive us as anti-social, narcissistic, and self-absorbed – which, in a way, we are at this time, but in the service of something beyond simple narcissism that is ultimately and profoundly pro-social.

"Selfish" and "self-centered" are terms we may hear or feel directed at us, and a part of us may agree with this negative judgment. Then feelings of guilt can derail us. Women in particular are prone to take such feedback as a reflection of something wrong with us, and we often give up our Star quest to compromise on something more congruent with our family and social roles. It seems more than coincidence that a lot of us who persist in following our FIVE calling also at some point find ourselves in divorce court. I have noticed, through many years of interacting with graduate students, a disproportionate number of women getting divorces as they get their doctorates or master's degrees – especially those women who had returned to school after a number of years as wives and mothers.

Women who are strongly drawn toward Center FIVE and even beyond but whose life, or simply the natural course of social development, inclines us toward marriage and motherhood, tend to experience a lot of push/pull feelings regarding our spousal and maternal roles, even when gladly and voluntarily chosen. On the one hand, Aloha strongly commits us to supporting our spouses and helping our children actualize themselves as the unique human beings they are, and we recognize the importance of being there for them. On the other hand, the call of the Seed is agitating for more attention and space to grow into its own form.

The result can be pervasive inner conflict regardless of which way we go, because the balancing act is so tricky. Creativity plays by its own rules and does not fit into a family schedule any more than it fits into a regular nine-to-five job schedule. How it chooses to come through varies with each individual, and while it can be cajoled and bent (sometimes) to accommodate our personal needs, it is essentially impersonal and flows in its own time and its own rhythm. We can dance with it, but we can't always lead. If it is to ripen and release its fruits, creativity has to be in charge of its own process.

This same tension exists for men, but their self-judgment and external feedback tends to center more around neglecting their obligations as providers, or other issues of "duty." The military term "dereliction of duty" comes to mind as a part of male socialization that is not confined to military service. On the one hand, fidelity to one's obligations and willingly assumed duties is a high virtue in anyone. When imposed as an outside or inside "should" in the face of a genuine "Seed call," however, it likewise becomes an obstacle to be faced with ethical discernment and wisdom, taking everyone's genuine needs into account and finding the best "win/win" solution possible.

The Tango cycle also tends to be a time of serious spiritual exploration. Our particular Star will inevitably be linked to our spiritual "path with heart," whatever that path turns out to be. Whether within an established tradition or something individually arrived at, it is likely to be of central importance in our lives. Whatever form we project onto the ultimate

Ground of Being, the Great Mystery, or however we name It, we are now relating to its transpersonal dimension. Yet we often find ourselves with insufficient time and/or energy to fully honor the centrality of this quest in our lives.

It is not a coincidence that historically, in all religious traditions, a serious commitment to spiritual practice usually required a monastic context, either permanently or temporarily. In contemporary culture, this is difficult and often impractical, especially if we are financially and/or physically responsible for other people, and finding ways to be monastic in the midst of daily living without the support and safe containment of a monastic environment is a major challenge, though not impossible. I have found being part of a spiritual community of fellow travelers on a similar path an invaluable inspiration and support on my own journey.

Another part of the undertow pulling us and holding us in Center TWO as we reach toward FIVE is generated from within – by our own emotional unfinished business from earlier developmental stages. Suddenly our family of origin may look different from the picture we have been carrying inside us. We may realize that this picture is far from the lived reality: that we have selected memory items to display in what I call our personal "Museum of My Past." These seemed important at the time we created the display, but may no longer be relevant or alive for us, except to the extent that we continue to infuse them with energy, whether positive *or* negative. We may also find old items in the basement of the museum that seem more relevant now, or find treasures and gifts we never realized were there.

In response to our need for authenticity, we find ourselves irresistibly drawn into dancing with our past, whether our partners turn out to be inner ghosts or real people. It is uncanny how, as we are launched into this process, all kinds of outer synchronistic events and people turn up in our lives and bring the old feelings and reaction patterns associated with them to the surface again. In any case, what we really dance with is our own complexes.

It helps a lot to recognize that. We created the meanings attached to the people and events in our museum that made them important enough to be displayed there, and we can now re-frame those meanings. To re-view our museum displays through our present lens of awareness inevitably modifies or even transforms the story we identified with as "my life" – a story we have taken to be the whole truth about "how it really was" and "what really happened." We recognize it as a story derived from our social matrix, internalized by us and re-shaped by Ego to reflect its own perceptions and projections. We find satisfaction in the clarity with which we now see and understand things that once were too obscure for our vision, or more painful or distasteful than we could bear.

The Descent Tango is a passionate dance, and yet, at least during those moments when our witnessing capacity is turned on and not submerged in the drama of the old choreography, also a joyful one. Without the witnessing presence, however, we may forget that we are now dancing on a much bigger stage than before, and that we have the power to re-choreograph our dance to suit who we are becoming rather than who we once were. If we forget this, we may start doubting whether we have made any progress at all.

In the words of a young mother of three, a very creative person who has chosen to stay home and give her children the consistent mother-presence that she herself did not have as the child of a busy professional woman,

> I currently feel like I am back in the trenches – tears, volatile emotions as though I've gone backward into neurotic adolescent self-doubt and lack of confidence. But I can feel the inner witness hovering above, waiting and watching, excited because I also sense a freedom from something,

*and that it will come...*

We are like the proverbial flies walking on an elephant and trying to figure out what sort of being this is. We know we are being moved by it, but we're not clear about where we are going. This is how it is at first. Then, in the full flush of Egoic energy, we are like the flies who think *we* are moving the elephant, and live in the delusion that we are controlling where it is going. At Center FIVE, we can get far enough for a more objective view and begin to see the outlines of the whole elephant, however dimly. We can then try to figure out if it might be going in our direction, and hitch a ride.

Of course, we have gone through this before, but from a different perspective. We may have felt a need at TWO or THREE for something "more," something with more meaning and purpose, but because of where we were experiencing *from,* we could only see through the lens of that Center. So we naturally used the energy of the Star Center within us to express ourselves within the boundaries of the Second Center's reality, and appropriately so. Now it is different. It is more than just a personal process.

What characterizes the descent phase from FIVE to TWO, assuming we have done adequate shadow work and arrived at a sufficient degree of self-acceptance, is a capacity and enthusiasm for conscious and non-judgmental self-witnessing. This is something we have developed at FOUR, and it is now solidifying as we expand into FIVE. The lens we look through is now bigger than the dance, and the conscious witness has its eyes open more of the time, and looks with a more compassionate eye. This is crucial, because without the bigger lens, we would not notice when the undertow of old perceptions and habits threatens to sweep us back into the same old patterns – and the same ego strivings.

With our new and bigger lens, and further informed by hindsight, if we can remain alert and if we have enough clarity about the Star we are following, we now have the capacity to choose. We can refuse to dance with some inner partners, invite others, change the music, choose the steps. We can face down the inner critic and discard outer criticism that our discernment has recognized as unwarranted. Earlier, before we got to this point, we tended to blame circumstances or other people for our unhappiness. Some of us who are prone to guilt played an endless self-blame game, as though we wouldn't have seen more clearly and done things better if we could have at the time. Now we take responsibility (response-ability) for our own complexes and emotional reactions.

The "I" has now become mostly an identifier for the witnessing consciousness that can empathize but does not identify with any of the voices from our neurotic drama. We realize that the emotions driving our complexes are like waves which build up, crest, and then dissolve back into the ocean, so if we manage to not react but just hold on and let them wash through, the emotions will pass. We will then be better able to deal appropriately with whatever gave rise to them.

We have learned that other people may indeed criticize us, try to push us around, abandon us, but it is only if we accept this with a victim mentality that we end up feeling helpless or inferior. Each situation does demand an appropriate response, of course, and we can learn from every experience, like when other people point out our shadow stuff to us and thereby do us a great service. At the same time, what they say has to be subjected to a non-judgmental assessment by our own inner wisdom.

Contemporary self-help literature abounds with ways to deal with emotional problems, relationship problems, sexual problems, and the endless ways in which cathectic issues play out in our daily lives, and such books can teach a lot about dealing with specific Kinship Center issues that we happen to be re-visiting. So can psychotherapy, preferably with someone who has had some personal experience with the return cycles.

It bears emphasizing that this FIVE to TWO return cycle is not an intellectual exercise. It feels very real and visceral. We do not objectively look at these experiences from the "heights" of FIVE. We are *in the soup*. If we are not, the descent is not genuine and we are trying to fabricate it just in our heads. It won't work. The emotional body has to participate, too. All of us does. Embodied experience is emotional and physical, as well as mental - and always spiritual, whether that is explicit or not.

There is a paradoxical double focus in this process, in which we *really dance* (sweat and all) while also witnessing the dance with compassion and without judgment, delighted at the realizations that enable us to see more clearly, understand more deeply, and live more consciously. Whether what we see is pleasant or not, whether the light shines on something beautiful or ugly, it is the light and the seeing that matter. The truth really does set us free.

The basic goal here is to shed all the encrusted, conventional beliefs and response patterns from our conditioned cathectic past that no longer support our being authentic in the present. The task for our developing consciousness is to distinguish what really fits our life here and now from what no longer does, or perhaps never did. We have all at times worn clothes that were too small or too big, the wrong style or the wrong color, nice clothes perhaps for someone, but not for us. This task is like clearing out our mental/emotional closets, our basement, our garage, our social relationships, our compulsions and ground-in thought patterns, so that we can finally have the space to live in our authentic psychological and spiritual house. This is inner clutter cleaning.

A woman I know got into a marriage during the early rounds of this descent in which she said that parts of her felt like they were being squeezed through a sieve, and what remained after everything else was squeezed out was a residue that re-formed her in some basic way that she experienced as deeply real.  At that point, she and her husband had no meaningful connection left, except on a purely practical worldly level, and she felt lonelier with him than alone.  Even some abstract values they still shared were now far apart in their lived meaning and application – Centers apart.

When they met, she was re-visiting unfinished emotional and sexual issues as part of a FIVE – TWO descent cycle.  At the same time, as a serious seeker for her authentic life purpose and spiritual path, she was also struggling with TWO to FIVE "ascent" challenges.  He, on the other hand, seemed to be retreating to TWO in a flight from the inner revolution required of the THREE to FOUR transition.  Accepting the invitation to dance the Aloha Waltz was the logically appropriate growth step for him, but too much for his Ego to tolerate.

Where they met was at Center TWO.  Passions ignited, cathexes meshed, and both fell "into the soup" of romantic intoxication. With hindsight, she realized that the relationship never had a chance, though neither of them was "wrong." They simply connected at a point in time and at a developmental nexus which was not "home" for either.  She was re-visiting Center TWO to deal with unfinished business that presented an obstacle to her Star path, while for him, the return served as an escape in the service of Ego.  For the long haul, they were wrong for each other, though the relationship was good for both of them at that time, even if only temporarily.

After more than a decade of intense ups and downs, a lot of both real caring and intense pain, the relationship ended without rancor on either side.  Both could see in retrospect many valuable inner and outer lessons learned from each other, and, from a Star perspective, she was able to honor the sincerity of their mutual attempt even as she grieved the loss. The pain passed; the learning remained.

While clearing our path to Center FIVE, especially if we are conscientious and truly care about the feelings of our significant others, there can develop an almost overwhelming tension between the horizontal axis of relational demands and the problem of our own psychological complexes on the one hand, and the vertical axis which pulls us onto a bigger stage and a new "play" on the other – one which is totally new to us.

If the feeling of tension gets strong enough, we may let ourselves be pulled back into familiar patterns, even if they no longer fit us, and try to close our eyes to the Star that keeps flickering in the periphery of our vision. Safety is very tempting when the alternative is the dark unknown, as well as possible alienation from our kinship circles. Yet once we have experienced the pull of the Star, it tends to stick around like a buzzing mosquito that keeps reminding us that we are not walking the path we were meant for. If we can recognize this as as a reminder of our Seed call, and realize that this struggle, too, *is* our path, we will see that anything else, though it may be superficially pleasant and worthwhile in a relative sense, is a detour, and that there is only one valid choice.

Spiritually, FIVE is the Center of the "Seeker." Unless we have found our home in a specific spiritual tradition, this stage is likely to bring both an intensification of yearning for some kind of transcendent connection, and confusion about how this connection might be realized. The ultimate Reality beyond the duality we live in may be glimpsed here as a "peak experience" or intuition, but not yet as felt reality. Most of us still want and seek a spiritual *Other* with whom to have a relationship: a personified deity or perhaps a spiritual teacher whose living example can embody it for us. And we also seek the support of a community of kindred spirits if we can find one.

The search for a spiritual home may lead some of us to wander through the spiritual marketplace readily available today in search of the "right" path and the "right" *Other*. This may come as a surprise if we had felt more spiritually settled earlier in our lives. Nature mysticism can have a strong appeal, too, as we find ourselves attracted to spiritual forms that are grounded in human community and "Mother Nature." Nature is a divine manifestation we can all relate to.

What we call secular humanism can also serve in this way as a popular contemporary form of compassionate inclusiveness. This is reflected in humanistic psychology and the human potential movement of the last quarter of the 20th century, which in spite of its individualistic focus saw equal growth potential in everyone, at least as a possibility. There are so many options and paths today promising self-realization that we are in danger of becoming spiritual dilettantes and never digging our well deep enough in one place to draw water from the Source we seek.

Because we long for the comfort of our earlier certainties, Ego may find ways to block our search, or co-opt the process for its own purposes altogether. When this happens, no path is acceptable as the "right" one because the unseen, unintegrated shadow elements still color our perceptions and undermine our commitment to *any* path.

Perhaps we commit to a particular path and become spiritually ambitious, trying hard to become "more enlightened-than-thou" faster than thou. Chogyam Trungpa Rinpoche, a well-known Tibetan spiritual master, called this "spiritual materialism." It is an easily observable phenomenon in contemporary spirituality, and a trap we can all fall into, and most of us serious seekers do at some point on our journey.

Paradoxically, the Star Center often calls to us through mystical and paranormal experiences. Such experiences may not fit our past notions of reality and may frighten some of us back into in-law reality unless we have some understanding of what these experiences mean, and don't mean. At their best, they can serve as a powerful validation of and inspiration for the journey we are on, as long as we recognize that "regression in the service of transcendence," with its inherent cycles, is still a natural part of our spiritual maturation process.

Psychic and paranormal experiences are particularly susceptible to Ego appropriation. We don't easily (if ever) outgrow the wish to be "special," and it is easy to assume that these experiences indicate a high level of spiritual attainment, or that we have powers that other people don't have. It is important to look for the meaning of spiritual experiences in the context of the whole journey, and mobilize the courage to continue without placing too much emphasis on the experiences themselves.

There are no "special" capacities in us that are not also in everyone else, though our capacity to perform in any specific area seems to have some inborn dimensions. How these capacities manifest depends on how conscious and developed they are in any given individual, and that is largely a function of effort and practice, like singing, a capacity we all have and can develop (barring a physical disability). At the same time, some were born with a good voice, work to develop it, and sing like Pavarotti, while, at the other end of the spectrum, some of us (like me) could not even sing acceptably in a choir no matter how hard we try. Ours is simply not a singing "Star," though we can enjoy singing as much as we like, if only in private.

Talents and highly developed skills that we consider special do not necessarily imply goodness, nor are they always used in the most compassionate and ethical ways. In the absence of genuine Aloha and a non-intrusive Ego, such abilities can also be used to harm, either consciously or through ignorance. This also applies to transpersonal and mystical experiences, which are, at their best, inspirational pointers to what is possible – "previews of coming attractions." As such, they can provide an impetus toward seeking wholeness and adopting a serious spiritual practice. All light casts a shadow – that is the nature of a dualistic world – but the shadows do not dim the light. They simply make the outlines of what the light shines upon more visible.

Those in traditional religions may now need time to restructure how they relate to the forms of their tradition, perhaps extending these forms to incorporate beliefs and practices from other traditions. This seems to be happening on an unprecedented scale today. Dogma becomes de-emphasized in favor of the living core of the teachings. Whatever our chosen path, lived experience of a transpersonal realm in some form is clearly a part of the full Star experience.

The Star Center (and even more perhaps, the transpersonal Centers next on the horizon) can also become an escape for those who attempt a "spiritual bypass," that is, an attempt to avoid the difficulties and challenges of full human development by escaping to levels of experience and practice that are seen as "higher" or "above" the "merely" human. We attempt an end-run around the human predicament in the hope that we can skip the challenges of ordinary every-day living by "transcending" the mundane and human.

We thereby also try to avoid the need to re-visit and unpack unpleasant "baggage" that needs our attention, and to avoid growth challenges that we are averse to. We refuse repeated invitations to the dances of return. That, too, then adds to the shadow baggage we carry, blocks our development as whole human beings, and will inevitably manifest unconsciously in dysfunctional and potentially harmful ways.

The denial and avoidance fueling by-pass also deprive us of the discovery of our "bright shadow" – our undiscovered and unlived potentials – which could be a source of renewal when we get stuck or stagnant. Focusing only on the spiritual and ignoring our psychological/emotional issues are strategies doomed to failure, yet their effects are often underestimated as obstacles to spiritual maturity. Discernment here requires both psychological and spiritual astuteness, not to mention honesty. Staying conscious in the face of Ego's attempts at resurgence is an ongoing ethical challenge.

For those of us who get caught in this pattern, understanding the FIVE - TWO return cycle is particularly relevant, because bypassed development eventually demands its due. To persist in resisting the descent is to get stuck in a one-sided pseudo-spirituality that is nothing more than an Ego-based masquerade.

Personal authenticity and a spontaneously creative response to what life presents are the fruits of a genuinely lived Star Center. In finding our own true "voice," we learn to sing in tune with the universal chorus. However, before this can come to fruition, we must have accomplished substantial return work – I say substantial because our characteristic patterns never completely disappear, only lose their power as we cease to identify with them. Having distilled whatever wisdom they can yield, we can now detach from the sticky "velcro" that keeps us in their hold. We can learn to let go even as we also let be, without clinging.

Grief is also a major theme of this return, often buried under anger, resentments, rationalizations, and denials. Depression is a frequent symptom of the need for this work to be done. At this point, we have to tell (at least ourselves) the truth about how it was and is, and embrace it all. "Yes, this too was a part of my life." "Yes, I did do that." "Yes, this is a scar that I will always carry." It is also a time, though, to appreciate anew our achievements, our joys, the moments of grace and communion, the unexpected gifts life has given us, and to celebrate these with gratitude. Simply being alive then becomes cause for celebration, because the future is open and invitingly fertile.

Gratitude is a remarkably life-giving feeling, and immediately immerses us in Spirit, whether we are aware of it or not. And a big part of the Descent Tango is for us to see with new eyes and gratitude this precious human life we have been given, with the gifts that have brought us to the stage of awareness where we are doing this work at all. Not all gifts came in pretty packages, of course. Some of our greatest learnings probably came from those that were not pretty. In retrospect, though, it all usually seems worthwhile.

In another step of the Descent Tango, we are called upon to finish unfinished business, gather the learnings we missed on earlier rounds, and also to fill in any remaining gaps in our experience at previous stages that are still important to complete. For example, we may feel we need to develop or refine social and relationship skills, or recognize and express our need for emotional intimacy, or re-activate our parental/nurturing capacities, or lend a helping hand in our community, or secure our financial base, or give our childlike playfulness more space in our lives, or whatever else will strengthen the foundation on which our life is now unfolding and fill the unfilled spaces of our wholeness.

It is also important to celebrate our embodiment and resolve unfinished issues relating to our sexuality and its expression, as well as physical and emotional problems that may lead to dysfunctional behavior, addictions, or other harmful behavior patterns. Early wounds from abuse can also come up again, or come up for the first time if they have not been dealt with earlier. It is a time of major purification and clearing, paradoxically painful and joyful at the same time.

There is much resistance to this return in most of us, especially those who have spent a lot of time in inner work, and perhaps years in therapy, dealing explicitly with family-of-origin and relationship issues. "Been there, done that!" pretty much sums up our reaction to this stuff that is in our face – again. We would like to dismiss this "re-call," but there is no way "up" but "down" first. This is difficult to reconcile with the genuine desire at this time to focus on our creativity and spiritual life. Return work seems so mundane and unappealing by comparison, especially if we have spent years in spiritual practices and had some powerful mystical experiences. There really is no up or down, of course, simply energy realigning itself in the service of greater awareness and integration. But that is hard to grasp while in the throes of the process.

The temptation to attempt spiritual bypass can become really strong here, but we can be aware that to fall into it would be detrimental to our psychological and spiritual growth. We must continue the dance, or stagnate. As we do, we also re-activate the Aloha Waltz, so that Ego reappears on stage, usually in more subtle and insidious forms than when it had the starring role. That means we always have to keep our eyes open for its machinations and remind it of its proper place in the scheme of things. A spiritual teacher, guide, transpersonal therapist, or friend who can serve as a clear mirror for our process can be very helpful here, and ever more so the farther we venture on our path.

A friend heavily engaged in the Descent Tango told me recently that she feels she could not have authentically done this Power/Love dance to any extent at all had she not been swept into the Descent Tango and the joys and shocks of wading through old emotional baggage at a deeper level than she had ever before imagined. She also feels that the crucial element in the deep psycho-spiritual inner work she has done recently was finding a spiritual path as solid ground to stand on during the psychic earthquakes she was going through, as well as the right (for her) therapist/guide to walk with her through the descent process.

I mention this because it might help you better understand your own weavings through this "map," and because it illustrates the individual variability of the model. A map is information, not an itinerary or fixed program of action. It is only a way-finding tool.


Once committed to the work of descent, we can engage in its tasks with the helpful executive energies of Center THREE within the steady compassion of Center FOUR. We will discover satisfaction, pleasure, and joy in the clarity with which we can now see the patterns and habitual behaviors of the past which, at the time we were identified with that stage of consciousness, were too obscure for us to see, or want to see.

This descent process may take a long time to complete, perhaps being the central task of a whole lifetime. And it may require knowledgeable help and supportive companions. To carry it through requires the development of a strong will – no longer the selfish "I want, I will" of the Ego, but a will aligned with the universal Flow, Tao, or, in Western traditions, Divine Will, as in "Not mine, but Thy will be done." What we seek is creative expression of our transpersonal essence in whatever form has heart and meaning for us and our individual talents permit.

The energy involved here is actually more broad than what

is usually meant by creativity. It is also generativity, in Erik Erikson's meaning of the term – the kind of creativity that passes on the impetus and seed for new forms to others and to succeeding generations, rather than only producing a current tangible result for oneself. It is essentially compassionate, and has its own inherent wisdom.

Please remember that our Star does not have to be bright or light up the whole sky. It simply has to shine steadily in and through us, even if the human world can't see it at all. Social norms and conceptual filters can block out a lot of light, and so we do not shine for others' viewing any more than the stars in the sky do.

With each sweep over past obscurations with the "broom" of Aloha and Star consciousness, things get a little clearer, so that from seeing bits and pieces of reality through a haze, we move toward seeing more brightly a bigger and more coherent picture. This allows us to live and act in our lives with greater discernment, authenticity, and energy. We can now see and follow our Star with more consistency. We react to problems with greater equanimity. We are becoming the unique beings we were born to be at the same time that we are feeling more and more an integral part of the eternal Lifestream.

We have a sense of coming home to ourselves, and this brings an inner peace that is a relief from the emotional twists and turns of the Tango. Yet as long as we live in a dualistic world, the dances always go on, whether on or off stage, though perhaps more quietly. That is the work of integration.

And then we may begin to discern the need to embark on, or more often get drafted by life into, the Sophia Task. This is the SIX to ONE return. I could also call it the "Sophia Swing" to maintain the dance metaphor, but it does not really fit here because it has more to do with stillness, receptivity, and integration than the rhythm and movement of a dance, though, in the service of integration, it will also "swing" us all the way back to the Survival and Cathectic Centers at deeper, more subtle levels, presenting us in the process with all the trailers of unfinished business from all the previous Centers. The goal of this process seems to be to consciously embody transcendence, which is the fulfillment of the Sophia Task of Center SIX.

Before we go on, though, let us reflect a little more on the current chapter:

- What do you see as your greatest gifts and talents? How are you using them? For whose benefit?
- What is your "vocation"? Where is "the place where your deep gladness and the world's deep hunger meet"?
- Can you describe your "Star"?
- What might it be if all things were possible? If physical, financial, and time limitations did not exist?
- What trailers from previous Centers might impede your following your Star, as best you discern it? What would have to change about you or your life to clear the way? Have you found an authentic spiritual path that feels right for you? Do you practice it? How conscientiously? How often?

# CHAPTER SIX

# THE SOPHIA TASK

## *Center SIX: Embodying Spirit*

If we dare to travel down the bridge from head to body, we may find our soul in the darkness and we may find the questions which will quicken her, opening every cell as we bring her into consciousness. Body becomes embodiment, sight becomes insight. Sophia, wisdom in the body, begins to move through soul. Soul experiences herself as part of Shekinah, the light in creation, the Bride of God. Matter, instead of being a dark cave, becomes the revelation of God's beauty. The heart becomes the bridal chamber where soul that lives in time and space opens to spirit that is detached from life and death. There Bride and Bridegroom love.

Marion Woodman, *The Ravaged Bridegroom*

This return cycle, which embraces all previous Centers and will therefore reactivate unfinished business at any of them, focuses on the task of bringing about an inner union of opposites as a step toward their ultimate transcendence into non-dual consciousness: spirit and matter, masculine and feminine, inner and outer, body and mind, and so on. This includes consciously befriending our feelings and issues around death, so that we can live comfortably with our mortality with neither avoidance nor preoccupation, seeing life and death as integral parts of an infinite, unending Flow, even as we learn to embrace life in the present more deeply than ever before.

The task now is to recognize matter as also fundamentally spiritual, and therefore to honor and serve Sophia as divine Wisdom embedded in all manifest form. It means honoring and fully inhabiting our impermanent, mortal body even as we simultaneously recognize ourselves to be living Spirit. We are asked to leave behind our rather arrogant sense of superiority toward the earth and the feminine that we have inherited from our patriarchal past. As we develop in ourselves the wisdom energy we call Sophia (or any other personification more familiar or meaningful to us), we may grow more and more into a seamless integration of all our aspects – body, mind, emotions, spirit – without Egoic investment in any of them, or even in the wisdom itself.

Using the language of alchemy, Jung speaks of this as the *coniunctio* or "mystic marriage," as poetically described above by Marion Woodman. I believe this to be a major individual and collective task for us all during this century. Perhaps such an integral experience of our immanent and transcendent nature as an inseparable whole can save us from the self-centered and short-sighted ignorance that drives our ravaging of the earth and each other.

This behavior is not necessarily deliberate. We simply act in accordance with our worldview, habitual perceptions, and conditioned responses. A civilized society is fragile. It relies upon our higher Centers for success and can be disrupted by eruptions unleashed from lower Centers. In a world where everyone is only hours away from everyone else and we all affect each other all the time, this can easily happen. As our civilization and its technology become more advanced, and our potential power becomes more encompassing, psycho-spiritual maturity becomes ever more necessary in order to use these advances wisely. It is no longer optional. It is a matter of survival, for all of us and for our planet.

The ultimate gift of this Center is embodied wisdom. At

the Star Center, we may have become focused on our creative activities in a way that narrowed the scope of our overall perspective and this could have led to an imbalance in favor of doing at the expense of being. The focus on doing may have been constructive and even necessary in order to accomplish the tasks we set for ourselves, but now, to fully secure our home base at Center FIVE, we need enough psycho-spiritual balance to discourage Ego from trying to re-build its castle around our creative work. This means persevering on our creative path, once found, with integrity and without being swayed by or attached to projected results and other people's acclaim or disdain.

Such balance becomes all the more important as we expand to Center SIX, where we must further stabilize and extend the fruits of the Star Center along both the vertical and horizontal axes of development. Vertical moves us toward spiritual wisdom and transpersonal development, horizontal to the full and conscious experience of our humanness in all its facets as they manifest at any Center. A harmonious, integrated life now becomes possible.

Although as we seek Sophia we still relate to Spirit mostly through symbolic dualistic forms and rituals, there is a dawning awareness of the ultimate non-duality of existence, although not yet the full experience. Nevertheless, the dichotomy of body and Spirit, mind and matter, sacred and profane, is dissolving, as their polar aspects are enfolded into a larger whole even as their relative everyday manifestations are dealt with on their own terms. Paradox is the language of this Center, and a seamless melding of ineffability and experienced groundedness increasingly its substance as we move toward Center SEVEN.

Psycho-spiritual wholeness *is* paradoxical. It means a self-identification that is universal but fully grounded and living in the here and now — simultaneously. I am all that is, and all of that is manifested in who I am here and now, in this particular situation, doing this particular thing, with these particular others. Because we live bodily in time and space, we can only embody the universal within the limitations of this time and space.

Development along the vertical and horizontal axes may or may not be in sync – and often is not. One of the reasons may involve spiritual bypass, which we have already discussed, but which may become particularly seductive here, all the more so if we sense uncomfortable issues we would rather not deal with clamoring for attention. There may also be practical limitations of opportunity, ignorance of existing possibilities, personal handicaps or illness, and so on. Up to this point, it was possible to proceed along our path in spite of trailers and vertical/horizontal imbalances, but this becomes much more difficult now. Because integration is at the core of this return cycle, it reactivates all the unintegrated trailers along the way.

Typical leftover issues recycling here relate to our physical incarnation, including sickness, death, physicality, possessions, and the fact of impermanence in general, as well as the paradoxical emptiness and fullness of Being in particular. We have to learn to "die" before we actually die physically, and to maintain a centered equanimity through all the losses and changes of life's "little deaths" as well as its blissful highs. This means honoring and fully inhabiting our mortal body with all its needs and glitches, as we also come to embody in ourselves a life wisdom embedded in our deathless Ground, no longer seeing them as separate.

Moving fully into Center SIX as our psycho-spiritual home would mean we feel fully grounded in the earth and in our bodies, yet do not identify with either. We have left behind most if not all of our fears and come to trust the greater Lifestream flowing through us, knowing It as us, and ourselves as It. We have learned to love generously, act spontaneously and compassionately, be comfortable in and appreciative of our life circumstances whatever they are, and accept people in general and our loved ones in particular with all their quirks and neuroses. Ourselves, too.

We have gone beyond interest in external power but exercise it with discretion when called for, and compete when appropriate without egoic investment in winning or losing as such. We express our inherent talents and spiritual values in a way that benefits others and harms none. This includes honoring our own needs and limitations as we honor those of others, loving "your neighbor as yourself," as Jesus exhorted us. Symbolically, we could visualize ourselves as a dancing sphere of rainbow light with the energies of all the Centers in harmonic sync, which, as we continue to mature spiritually, gets brighter and brighter. This image may not describe us yet, appearing only as a nebulous possibility on a far-off horizon, but we may have occasional experiences of this kind as "previews of coming attractions," inspiring us to persevere.

It is the nature of Spirit to move into form: to person-ify. What we speak of as Soul – personified Spirit – is our name for that which holds the tension between spirit and matter, having the ability to be either and both. Soul is experienced as personal, while Spirit is transpersonal. When Soul loses itself in Spirit, it becomes ungrounded and out of touch with the total person's legitimate earthly needs. While losing itself in matter and those same needs, it separates itself from its ultimate nature as Spirit. Soul thrives on the balancing point where these two polarities meet, in what is truly the transcendent dance of Sophia.

SIX is obviously not a heavily inhabited home Center,

and the journey here is a long and necessarily demanding one. Sages and truly wise ones who live here are rare. The ones who do often tend to be relatively invisible, living simply and most often engaged in tasks that do not call attention to themselves. An example from my own experience is a Catholic priest, recently deceased, whose Zen name was Hando. He very quietly, over many years, built bridges between Buddhism and Christianity, softened sectarian dogmatism in his students of both traditions, and inspired hundreds of meditators to mature both in their spiritual practice and their everyday humanity. I include myself in this number.

Externally, wise ones usually (with some eccentric exceptions perhaps) appear no different from their neighbors inhabiting other Centers, except that on closer acquaintance they emit a quiet light and an inner peace which rubs off on others. They have a presence that is hard to define but palpable. Their thinking is definitely "out-law," but they do not proclaim their knowledge or opinions without being invited to do so, and even then with discretion. If their Star has led them to teach or to become known in a way that brings visibility or even celebrity, they still tend to be modest and ordinary in their everyday behavior.

One of their core characteristics seems to be what is called, in various traditions, sacred outlook, sacramental vision, or pure vision, which refers to seeing through the chaos and suffering on the surface of life into the clear light of Spirit as the essence of everything – seeing Christ or Buddha or God in everyone and everything regardless of outer appearances. They also embody personal authenticity, kindness, and simplicity, and invariably have a spacious sense of humor. The prevalent manifestation of such qualities in all the Tibetan lamas I met first attracted me to Tibetan Buddhism, which is now my spiritual home. Even the Dalai Lama, whose realization obviously exceeds that of Center SIX, refers to himself as a "simple Buddhist monk." And I am told he really means that.

I have found similar qualities in all the genuine spiritual teachers I have encountered, regardless of religious affiliation, especially the joyful sense of humor. Their teaching does not lie primarily in the words they speak or the profound insights they impart, which can be priceless, but rather in their own being and presence. They are examples of what I mean by embodied spirituality. However, most of the rest of us still have a complex task ahead, in this case the most encompassing and subtle of the return cycles, which might announce itself thus:

**Before inhabiting this Center, you must re-integrate Center ONE, as well as leftover trailers from other Centers. You must fully and mindfully inhabit your body in the here and now: physically, mentally, emotionally, and spiritually. This will require using all the gifts of skill and wisdom gleaned from all previous Centers.**

The Sophia Task is actually a misnomer. It is not really a task that *we* do. *It* does *us*. It is really not a *doing* at all, but a dissolution process in which we cooperate: a shedding and releasing of everything Ego has clung to, especially what we have thought of as our identities. We do not practice; we are practic*ed*. We do not transform; we are transformed. We do not integrate; we are integrat*ed*. It feels like successive layers dropping off or withering away: a voluntary letting go into the "little deaths" I mentioned earlier.

Despite the jolt to our sense of permanence as our "self" dissolves into what feels like a boundless void, we also feel relief and a sense of belonging and serenity that exceeds anything we were able to create for the separate self no matter how hard we tried. We don't have to "hold it together" any longer, because there is no separate "it" and it was never *not* together. We are simply a wave in an ocean that can never reject us and will always support us, because it *is* us and we are *it*. So what is there to be afraid of?

Our choice is to stay awake and go with this process, or flee. The latter course results in a bumpy ride. To really feel and know how ordinary we are, just like everyone else despite our genuinely unique Star qualities, may seem frightening at first because it erases the "special" self-image Ego has striven for and identified with as real and solid. We may have needed it as part of our development, but now we have outgrown it, which may take a while to sink in.

Our progress here can be easily disrupted in its early stages by a reactivated Aloha Waltz shifting back to Ego's leadership –"Wow! Look how enlightened I am getting."–or Ego's fear – "This is all fine, but it's not real life. Let's get our feet back on the ground." Then Center FIVE achievements may be derailed into Ego trips, precipitating a regression that reshuffles relationships among all the Centers as we shrink into our fears. This makes everything we do more of a struggle, and may also precipitate depression, anxiety, and a variety of physical symptoms. Sophia's light is then dimmed or once more buried.

One of the biggest triggers for retreat to previous Centers is the need at this time to face our fears and issues around death, others' and our own: our tendencies toward denial, distraction and avoidance, or its complement of sugar-coated naivete (simply another form of avoidance and denial), which is evident in some contemporary concepts about death. If we are to be whole, we must come to recognize and embrace death in life and life in death, without overreacting to either or fearing either.

Equanimity is a gift of wisdom. Our essence knows there is no separation, no beginning or end to the great flow of Life, but Ego, which is born from the survival instinct, finds its own death unacceptable, perhaps inconceivable. Even if it intellectually accepts the idea of death, when we observe our minds closely, we may realize that Ego still subtly harbors the notion that it will go through death and proceed intact into rebirth or to heaven or whatever its end-of-life image is – *as itself in its present form*. In other words, Ego fully intends to attend its own funeral.

This is an implicit assumption hard to dislodge, but when dislodged, we reach a spiritual turning point, much like when our proverbial fish first sees beyond water. As we did then, we must now again choose to either integrate this new view and expand our heart-mind to include it, or turn away from the Sophia Task and cling to the old worldview preferred by Ego. The body's life processes also instinctively fight their diminution and cessation. These, too, are realities we must face, until we truly know ourselves *as* the Flow of life and death in our continuity through both, without need of the identity we are currently living through.

The revered Sixteenth Karmapa, acknowledged as one of the greatest Tibetan Buddhist masters of the 20th Century, exemplified this level of realization when he smilingly told students at his deathbed: "Nothing happens," expressing total comfort in what, from the point of view of the eternal Lifestream, is a non-event. Though he, of course, far exceeded the scope of Center SIX consciousness, he points us toward what we are also capable of realizing.

Approaching the Sophia Center – paradoxically in the light of what has just been said about shedding and letting go rather than doing – we now have serious psycho-spiritual work to do. Embodiment is in the details. Someone going through this return cycle can superficially appear very involved with what, to those who equate spiritual with ephemeral or otherworldly, may seem like trivial concrete issues. Yet they are far from trivial. All kinds of trailers from previous return cycles and the unfinished business of any of the other Centers can, and will, show up on-stage and add unexpected challenges to our current life drama which have to be met.

Yet all the while, that luminous Essence from which everything arises and to which everything returns shines through it all, and Sophia's gift is that we can now see it, at first "through a glass darkly" and then with more and more clarity. Sort of like windshield wipers sweeping across a muddy windshield, clearing the glass a little more with each sweep until all the dirt and fog have been washed away.

Unexpectedly, the body can become a demanding and trickster-like teacher in this process, producing sometimes vague and shifting symptoms leading to unclear or mistaken diagnoses and unsuccessful treatment attempts. The person involved and the health care professional trying to help may both feel as though they are shadow boxing, and a frequent conclusion can be mutually projected blame for the lack of expected results, or for the health professional to label it all "psychosomatic." This label has been used to mean anything from "It is all in your head, it is not real," to a more realistic but still vague attribution to "stress" without being able to define either cause or cure.

This scenario can happen at any stage of our journey, but often, during this particular return cycle, such a situation turns out to be a necessary and beneficent purification process once it is recognized as such. Such recognition does not deny the physical reality of the illness, but simply validates the inseparability of the body-mind continuum and calls for a multi-faceted approach encompassing all aspects of the person. What follows is a first-hand account by my close friend and spiritual sister Beverly Gorsuch, eloquently describing some aspects of the Sophia Task. I am deeply grateful to her for sharing it.

When I was young I believed that when I became an elder I would either have it all together or I would be a dried up prune – both static conditions. Instead, to my surprise, delight (and sometimes dismay), I found that with every approaching year I was propelled into an accelerating growth process. This was especially true at age sixty-nine when I was severely injured and looked infirmity, perhaps even death, in the eye. Now at age seventy-four, continuing to heal from this injury, I find myself in the midst of the most dynamic, adventurous, sometimes scary and rewarding time of my life.

In many ways my experience can be likened to a lengthy near-death process, a spontaneous total-life review seen not through the opinionated, alternating self-righteous and self-abnegating neurotic eyes of my little self but through the eyes of God, the eyes of my soul. This is a seeing of my life which is a radical blend of truth and compassion. "And you shall know the truth and the truth shall make you free."

It's as though I have a loving yet unrelenting searchlight inside myself which with great precision is illuminating every nook and cranny. The Light is searching for any residue of traumas, resentments, grudges, envy, jealousy, fears, griefs, sorrows, self-pity, superiority, inferiority, and despair. When these are found and illuminated the Light softens and becomes gentle, giving me the space and courage I need to enter and meet whatever is there.

Although most of these explorations are in old familiar territory, visited many times over the years, sometimes I still find myself narcissistically offended: "Surely not!" or "What? I took care of that years ago!" Or even, "I took care of that last week." Most of these visitations have softened with each meeting but some haven't, and a few are extraordinarily slippery, even devious, sliding under rocks or behind boulders as the Light approaches. And some of my patterns and rigidities have a sense of humor, taunting me with the illusion that I can never catch them or that I even need to.

Exploring my life-long patterns and rigidities is the most difficult work. Rather than hiding away in a corner of my psyche, these templates are intricately woven into the very cells of my body. They masquerade as an essential life force. It takes a very determined and discriminating eye to see that these rigidities are a part of a false self, and even then I pause, "Surely my very foundation will crumble if I look at them clearly." I hesitate, almost bolt, and ask myself the necessary questions: "Can I look at what's coming without my self-esteem being shattered? As Anne Michaels asks in *Fugitive Pieces*, can my "humility grow larger than [my] shame?" The challenge as I go forward to meet negative, painful memories, emotions, restrictive patterns and suffering, is whether I can stay with them, savoring and tasting and reliving their <u>full</u> overwhelming intensity.

If I do stay with them, the mystery – the absolute wonder – is that I am taken to an entirely different place. A different consciousness comes in, of silence, of peace, of safety, sometimes joy, for there is nothing to hide, most of all from myself. I retrieve my own history and I become more whole. Increasing inner freedom comes with every integration – the childish with the mature, the lower with the higher, the human with the divine, the particular with the cosmic. I experience increasing authenticity, and a growing appreciation for the warm, generous forgotten memories that follow the painful ones. The true self, the soul, expands, evolves, and takes charge of this incarnation. In this process I come to know that Love is the basic core of the universe. Love is the Power, the evolutionary Force that expands, differentiates, and unites the cosmos and everything in it. It brings our disowned parts together making us authentic and whole, more able to give our own beautiful, flawed selves to the tapestry of Life.

Surprising outer events and especially the striking "coincidences" of everyday life which Jung called synchronicities seem to become more frequent at this time, and these can become markers and guideposts for us if we learn to use them as such. We must now learn to surrender, with discernment, to the waves and currents of the great Lifestream that we are and that our little life waves provide with a particular form and flavor. We recognize the need to honor these forms, just as we honor the great stream Itself as well. We learn that opposites cannot be reconciled at the level of consciousness on which they are experienced, but can be encompassed and integrated into a more spacious span of mind.

Spiritual practice is essential now, in whatever form most skillfully nourishes our ability to be wisely present, compassionately aware, and appropriately responsive. These qualities are essential to the Sophia Task. While optional for purely personal development, in the sense that we could live our lives quite effectively on a personal level without much development of these qualities beyond what our kinship context requires, transpersonal development cannot happen without them. Concepts alone will not do. We have to *know* in the sense of *gnosis,* with our whole being down to our cells. We have to embody what we know. And the body, too, can lead us to that knowing.

Every experience is then spiritualized, as in the following quote by my dear friend and colleague Rosemarie Anderson, a long-time spiritual practitioner in both the Buddhist and Christian traditions, whom I see as genuinely engaged in the Sophia task. For her, love and sex and egolessness came together in a relationship that felt vividly embodied yet ineffable – a rainbow of being in a transpersonal Flow that encompassed everything and yet, she said, was difficult to articulate.

Life is bigger now. What was inside seems outside, and outside seems inside of me. So I end up feeling like one of those Chinese brush-paintings with a little man down in the corner under a tree. The little man checks my email, gets estimates to fix my roof, and drives my car. But he's a sweet servant, my ego mind, taking care of life's nuts and bolts. A bigger me is surrounded by an immense landscape and airy space.

I've done two decades of spiritual practice and read numberless spiritual books, but still I stuck to believing that life events animate from themselves, that they happened to me, that they existed in a separate way from me – distinct, objective, and outside. I used to think that I could fix things, change things. But now thought and events that ought to be paradoxical have space around them; they don't collide. Now the landscape, the space, and the little man seem too as one undivided whole. Each flows freely from one unseen source.

What is the source? Perhaps it's my beloved–like Joseph's touch.

At least – and finally – I know I don't know. For certain this bigger sphere is far better and more lovely than the world of control and fix, manipulate and fix. I don't want to go back to that narrow world – ever. I'd rather live now in this uncertain sphere. This sphere of not knowing.

Does unshackling from the dream of this world unwind from here? I feel more free to act as the moment chooses me. I don't know. I don't know.

Comfort in living with "I don't know" (in the way we usually think of as knowing) is yet another fruit of this Center. I think most of us have had moments of wordless embodied insight – so-called "flow" experiences touch on that – and it is important that we recognize these as pointers to what is possible for us as something natural and constant in our everyday life. In her case, this is happening, perhaps reflecting a shifting "home base" toward Center SIX.

You will also notice in the above journal entry an absence of missionary spirit, which is another characteristic of this Center. No longer driven to improve upon what is, on the assumption that we know better, we may still do our best to change things when life and compassion invite us to, but we do them without investment in outcome. What we have called Ego is involved mainly as executor of the action rather than its energy source – like the little man in the painting described above. That's the embodiment part: to use our skills in the world in an appropriate and caring way for the benefit of all, not just for "me and mine" (who are, of course, still included), and without making it a big deal.

We have to do our part or our growth process stops, and our part is to practice. Spiritual practice that embraces our whole being and furthers our psycho-spiritual maturity does not consist of meditation and contemplation alone, though these are essential. Our essence is at home in silence and stillness, but our human wholeness and its expression in the world have their claim on us, too.

Lama Surya Das, a well-known American-born teacher of Tibetan Buddhism, emphasizes what he calls six pillars or building blocks of a spiritual life, not just for his own students but for any serious practitioner on any spiritual path. I see them as imperative for those engaged in the Sophia Task but no less desirable for anyone interested in spiritual growth. This may seem daunting at first in the context of our already busy lives, but when we do manage to integrate them into a consistent practice (even if imperfectly), they will become simply a part of the fabric of our days and reward us with more than we could ever have hoped. At least, that has been my own experience.

I have summarized these foundational practices below from notes taken during Lama Surya's teachings.

### Six Building Blocks of a Spiritual Life

1. Daily individual spiritual practice, such as meditation, prayer, *lectio divina,* mindfulness practice, chanting, and mantra repetition.

2. Spiritual study, such as the reading spiritual books, attending lectures, taking courses, and keeping a spiritual journal.

3. Personal growth work, such as psychological study,

introspection, psychotherapy, creative expression, as well as healthy lifestyle practices such as good nutrition, exercise, and energy balancing disciplines such as yoga, Tai Chi, and Chi Kung.

4. Group practice and spiritual companionship. Having a spiritual community of fellow travelers and the support of spiritual friends.

5. Learning from and practicing with spiritual teachers and mentors. Drawing on the wisdom of our spiritual elders. Ideally, having a personal mentoring relationship with a qualified elder or teacher of our chosen tradition.

6. Serving the larger community, and extending our circle of care to all beings, starting with those closest to us. Acting with mindfulness of our interdependence. Ecological living.

These are all practices that will help to integrate all the Centers and, done sincerely and consistently, will eventually lead to the full flowering of the Sophia Center – and beyond. The examples given here are general guidelines, not specific prescriptions. The first three are mostly private, done alone. The other three are more relational and/or communal. All together, they contribute to the kind of integral development that is being asked of us during this stage of our journey.

The Sophia Center can be thought of as the first truly transpersonal Center, and moving into it as "home," even in its first tentative phase and with the return cycles still in high gear, constitutes an irreversible shift in our worldview from personal to transpersonal. Allowing for our humanness and inevitable "slippages," once this shift stabilizes, however, it is no longer possible to genuinely return to an Ego-based reality.

Before presenting you once more with end-of-chapter questions to reflect upon, I also want to share with you three slogans I have adopted for myself which are providing much grist for the mill of both contemplation and practice:

1. Accept suchness. Embrace everything. Reject nothing. Accept what is, as it is, without labeling, judging, giving it a "spin" based on hopes or fears, or projecting stories and explanations onto it. The more clearly I see, the more wisely, mindfully, and skillfully I can respond – or choose not to respond.

2. Karma *is* Dharma. My life as it is (not as I might wish it) *is* my path. What happens in my life is largely not up to me, but how I respond is always up to me. Everything is potentially workable in the context of wisdom and compassion, and there is nothing we cannot learn and grow from. Pain is inevitable, but suffering is not. Pain happens to all of us; suffering comes from what our minds do with it and the stories we spin around it.

3. The truth (of who we really are) *shall* set us free. The truth I am referring to here is that we are not our Egos. We are so much more than either life or death or what happens to us in between, and who we really are does not suffer or change through any of our concrete, time-bound experiences. As an experienced reality, this perspective is the fruit of authentic and usually long-term practice within any tradition designed to promote enlightenment and, whether it stays or not, it can also come upon us suddenly, as an extraordinary blessing.

I leave it to you to unpack these further for yourself, if they resonate with you. If not, you can create your own, to fit your current path and practice. And now, as a start in doing that, some more questions for you to dance with:

- What dimensions of opposites are you struggling with? In your body? Your psyche? Spiritually?
- What are you still strongly attracted to or repelled by?
- Do you experience a dichotomy between mind and body? Psyche and spirit? Daily life and spirituality? Are there moments when the dichotomy dissolves? If so, what facilitates such moments?
- How do you relate to the concrete physicality of the world around you?
- Do you feel that you have found your life's meaning and purpose, or are you still seeking? What would "finding" look like?
- What spiritual practices and/or beliefs sustain you?
- Finally, who are you, really?

# CHAPTER SEVEN

# EMBODIED TRANSCENDENCE

*Center SEVEN: The Transpersonal Journey*

The Tao that can be told is not the eternal Tao.
The name that can be named is not the eternal Name.

*Tao Te Ching*

As suggested by the above quote, this chapter leads into spiritual territory that cannot be described in words, and yet it contains all the other Centers and everything that has gone before. In this model, Center SEVEN is not really *a* Center at all, but a condensation of many advanced stages of transpersonal development up to non-dual realms transcending all images, polarities, and descriptors. Although I am not qualified to do so myself, words pointing to what these realms are like from those who speak from first-hand experience can inspire us to persevere on our journey, and I shall share some that have inspired me. The rest is derived from the teachings I have received and tried to practice. It will therefore be a relatively short chapter, completing the map and taking us to the threshold of its final destination. A signpost as we approach this Center might read something like this:

**There are many levels at and beyond this Center, and to move into them in an authentic way, unless you are one of the rare ones who is already there, you need a solid and authentic spiritual path and practice, as well as a qualified**

**teacher or mentor.**

It is important to know that during these transpersonal stages as described in spiritual literature, especially the many Tibetan Buddhist texts recently translated into English, our "home base" returns to and settles into Center FOUR at the level of the awakened, "enlightened" heart-mind – active, unconditional compassion inseparable from wisdom. Buddhists call this absolute Bodhicitta, which describes the essence of Buddhahood and is the source of spontaneous enlightened activity in the world. In Christianity, we may refer to it as the fully awakened heart of the Risen Christ, the essence of Jesus' teaching and practice. The mystical contemplative paths within all spiritual traditions have their own ways of describing this same Essence, but in the language of this model, we can now think of the deepest level of the Aloha Center with all the others lit up around it, beaming love and blessings in all directions, all ways, not separate from anything.

Thus Center FOUR, through which in some way all the paths of our journey have passed, can be seen as both transitional and terminal. The way I think of it is that we circumambulate what we are until we fully recognize It, and then finally become It. That full becoming is the process of Center SEVEN. Our circumambulation becomes a dance of awake/aware Aloha – beyond Ego or *me* or *mine*.

Fr. Bede Griffiths, a saintly priest who lived in India and harmoniously blended the two traditions of Hinduism and Catholicism, had this to say in *A New Vision of Reality*:

> The importance of integration is often misunderstood, and it is frequently thought that, on reaching the level of non-dual awareness, everything disappears and there is simply pure identity of being... without any differentiation. But the truth is

that all the lower levels of consciousness have to be taken up into the Supreme and that is what constitutes total realization, that is, realization of the total reality... When we enter... a higher, more subtle level of consciousness... we discover the eternal realities behind the forms. But now we can go beyond the ideas into the Godhead itself, the Ultimate, and there all is gathered together in the One. And for this One, there are no words.

And Tibetan master Dudjom Rinpoche, describing this elusive ultimate Reality:

> No words can describe it
> No example can point to it
> Samsara does not make it worse
> Nirvana does not make it better
> It has never been born
> It has never ceased
> It has never been liberated
> It has never been deluded
> It has never existed
> It has never been nonexistent
> It has no limits at all
> It does not fall into any kind of category.

Jesus, speaking simply and directly from His own lived experience, put it very succinctly: "I and the Father are One."

Final transcendence takes us into this realm of ultimate non-duality, which is the pinnacle aspiration of all spiritual paths, regardless of what words or signposts we use as pointers. And it is right here, right now. There is simple *Is*-ness, also called *Suchness*. Everything else is human creativity and cultural commentary. Descriptions of this *Is*-ness are usually couched in terms like "neti, neti" ("not this, not that"), because words are inherently dualistic. Only non-conceptual awareness can access the non-dual – because such awareness is, itself, non-dual. *We* don't *have* this awareness; we *are* this awareness. Before it can dawn, however, we must first realize and become comfortable with what is often referred to as the Void, or emptiness, as the ultimate Ground from which everything arises and to which everything returns, in cycles without end.

This is how Dilgo Khyentse Rinpoche, another enlightened Tibetan Buddhist voice from the late 20th century, explains it in *The Heart Treasure of the Enlightened Ones*:

> The view of voidness has to be first understood, then experienced, and finally realized. It is from voidness that samsara and nirvana arise, and into voidness that they dissolve. Even while they appear to exist, they have actually never departed from voidness. So, if you recognize all phenomena as being void in nature, you will be able to cope with whatever happens, whether you experience pleasure or pain, without any clinging.

Yet this voidness (*sunyata* in Sanskrit) is at the same time a cognizant, unimpeded, luminous fullness imbued with Aloha, having the creative potential to manifest absolutely anything and everything. And it is nowhere other than in each and every living being, in all of us, every moment. Since it is our Essence, where else could it possibly be? We only have to awaken to it. Fr. Thomas Keating, a prime mover in the contemporary revival of contemplative practice within the Christian tradition, expressed it thus in a 2004 Christmas mailing:

> We open our awareness to the Ultimate Mystery whom we know by faith is within us, closer than breathing, closer than thinking, closer than choosing – closer than consciousness itself. The Ultimate Mystery is the ground in which our being is rooted, the source from whom our life emerges at every moment.

Here, at the Transpersonal Centers (using the plural again because of the many layers of possible realization condensed here for the purposes of this model) we will become more and more present in the now, and more and more free of any previous conditionings. We are still practicing, of course, but sustaining more often and longer the mystical state described above that is beyond any verbal or symbolic descriptors: "not this, not that" and yet everything. Though indicated but not really explained by suggestive terms like Pure Presence, Divine Union, Cosmic Consciousness, Naked Awareness, Innate Essence, Spontaneous Wakefulness, Rigpa, etc., it is our eternal source and destination, never *not* present, yet not easily recognized by us because we are so caught in the dualistic realm of our senses and mental constructs.

In this Center, we have passed irrevocably from personal to transpersonal in our worldview, and our *trans*personal journey becomes our everyday life. What might this life be like? It would flow spontaneously and without mental or emotional impediments anywhere on the "map." It could be described by terms like now-ness, conscious embodiment, discernment without judgment, generative creativity for the benefit of others and future generations, and above all, unfailing kindness. In the statement, "My religion is kindness," the Dalai Lama expresses such a life in the simplest possible way.

Whatever we call, or however we conceive of, ultimate awakening, some part of us knows it already and has experienced moments of grace or insight which may have prompted us to commit to a spiritual path and practice in the first place. This implicit knowledge is wired into our being, however deeply buried and however infrequently surfacing into consciousness. Jung called it the archetype of the Self that is inherent in the human psyche. To honor this, he carved in stone over the entrance to his home, in Latin: "Called or not called, God is present."

For some of us, such awareness may already have become a regular occurrence, or practice, or even our "home base," in which case the map provided here is no longer relevant, although it may still be interesting to look back on the road already traveled.  Except for the very rare few to whom this applies, however, for the rest of us there is always more to understand, some old or freshly created obscurations and neurotic habits to deal with, an ongoing journey and practice projected into infinity.  Yet always, there is also that inner light beckoning us to recognize and live out of our true nature. Spirit is matter-ing right here, right now, wherever we are.

Some time ago, as I was meditating in the forest, away from "civilization," I suddenly knew, without words but as simply so, that I could sit right there on that spot for the rest of my life and learn everything essential there is to know simply by blending into my surroundings.  Life was pulsating all around and through my body, waxing and waning in the trees, clouds, insects, birds, critters seen or only sensed, wind – everything!  No difference, simply so.  I don't know for how long, because this was out of time.  Then I noticed my watch, abruptly returning to the world of sequential time and the need to not be late for an appointment.  But the experience stayed with me and imbued my subsequent moments of relaxing in nature with a touch of pure Being.  There is no reason why the moments of my daily life and its tasks could not all be such sacred moments, and someday they will be.  Maybe even later today, or tomorrow.  I live in the not knowing, in the mysterious ongoing dance of Sophia.

To end our tour of the Centers and return cycles through which our process of becoming wends its way toward the maturing of simple Being, here are some final questions to contemplate:

- How do you envision "enlightenment"? Is there someone who, for you, personifies it?
- If you have had experience of such a being or beings, what was it like? Did it change you? If so, how?
- What is your own image or sense of the Ultimate Mystery?
- What if there really *is* only the fertile Void, which births each moment as it arises, and we really do exist only in this moment? Would that change you and how you live your life?

# CHAPTER EIGHT

# PERSPECTIVES ON THE PATH

*Reflections on Gender, Resonances, Detours,
and Body-Mind Connections*

The way we conceive of and relate to Spirit as we grow and develop into adulthood is likely to mirror our psychological patterns of human relations, especially through the first three Centers.  I believe we recapitulate these patterns in various forms as we shift to different Centers.  Some of us will "visit" Aloha, fewer will live there; fewer still will fully actualize their Star, and the Sophia Center is sparsely inhabited indeed, not to mention the transpersonal Centers.  Even the genuine sages who do live among us are often anonymous, except for those beneficiaries of their light with whom they have direct contact and who recognize them.

Practically speaking, then, it is up to the growing number of psycho-spiritually maturing people going through the Waltz and Tango cycles to tip the balance of global greed, hatred, and ignorance toward the necessary shift in consciousness that will help us survive on this planet.  Conventional psychology is of minimal help once the issues of the "out-law" Centers emerge (although this is now slowly changing), and those on a spiritual journey need validation and guidance as they follow the pathways toward their ultimate destination.  Some of the more common patterns and preferred pathways will be the subject of this chapter.

## Yin and Yang

The dance of the opposites – especially the polar energies we call masculine and feminine – is an important phenomenon throughout the Centers, now pulling more toward one, now toward the other, sometimes holding in balance. Several distinctions might be helpful here.

First, masculine and feminine in this context refer to complementary energies within both men and women that are wholly interdependent. They do not describe gender as such, although we are now finding some hormone-related tendencies that do seem to be biologically gender-based and reflect aspects of the common wisdom that has been popularized in the "men are from Mars, women from Venus" descriptions. To the extent that we each embody more or less of both of these energies, it is not surprising to find differences in how each of us travels through and uses them at the different Centers, and where we feel more or less comfortable.

"Masculine" energy is traditionally associated with a more active, externally focused, analytical, goal-directed orientation, and "feminine" with more organic, internal processes with a relational, feeling-based and nurturing focus. Also, masculine attention tends to be more focused, and feminine more diffuse and contextual. The action-based heroic archetype has been associated with the masculine, wisdom and nurturing with the feminine. The dance of these opposite energies goes on equally in men and women, with varying proportions of the two depending on the individual, and shifts back and forth.

Centers ONE, THREE, and FIVE – the Survival, Egoic, and Star Centers – seem to lean more toward the masculine, and TWO, FOUR, and SIX – the Kinship, Aloha, and Sophia Centers – toward the feminine. This means that, as we use these complementary energies and move from one Center to another, we will feel more or less comfortable and capable, depending on how well we are able to mobilize the qualities that are called for. Some of us are also more comfortable shifting gears and navigating transitions than others, and therefore more likely to explore new options than those who are more comfortable with what is familiar. This affects our openness to new perspectives, especially "out-law" ones.

Second, whether due to personality factors, wired-in hormonal effects, temperament, social conditioning, or pervasive habit patterns, we all have specific preferences and avoidance tendencies. We will tend to do the minimum required to get by in our least preferred areas and try to create our life where we feel more comfortable, which is not necessarily where our growing edge is – or where our inner Star may be beckoning. Therefore, we will more readily adapt to the tasks of some centers and prefer to slide by or skip if possible the tasks of others, thereby creating trailers that will persist in some form until we deal with them.

Third, the way men and women typically travel these pathways is obviously affected by cultural patterns. For many men, for instance, developing the Survival Center, especially in its aspect of physical strength and skill, seems to be essential to their basic sense of masculine competence and identity. In some pre-industrial societies, it can still be a matter of actual physical survival, and men who fail to develop the appropriate skills lower their status in their peer group. Today, sports and physical labor, as well as military training, can provide this kind of foundation, but this is optional because many mental rather than physical areas of competition and competence are available and socially rewarded, often more highly than physical skills.

Yet, we cannot totally escape our history. Even in the 21st century, men who fail to develop an adequate sense of physical competence and survivability may later have problems with self-esteem, and may try to compensate for this by over-developing Center THREE and over-investing in its criteria of success as measures of their masculinity and self-worth. Depending on how healthy a path this compensatory development takes, the result can be anything from a high level of positive achievement and productivity to a relentlessly power-driven Ego.

Women, on the other hand, may hardly deal with survival skills at all, but settle easily into the Kinship Center and the role of nurturer, social networker, and homemaker universally assigned to them, even in our own culture and even if they also hold down jobs. This, and the engrossing practical realities of having and raising children, can lead to a necessary dependency on others that generates a sense of insecurity and fear of being abandoned, sometimes resulting in what we call "co-dependency."

A woman can usually opt to stay in the safe, or at least familiar, cocoon of Center TWO and develop only those Egoic skills that serve their cathectic orientation. This socially sanctioned "cocooning" was, until the mid-twentieth century, the norm and measure of women's mental health. We tend to embrace or disown certain tasks and behavior patterns depending on whether we perceive them as culturally sanctioned for our gender or not, and many women chose to force themselves into this norm whether it fit them or not, until Betty Friedan's book *The Feminine Mystique* coined the term "the problem that has no name" for the plight of such "misfit" housewives – and started a cultural revolution.

Even in the Sixties, when I decided to enter a demanding doctoral program full time as a mother of two very young children, I ran into disapproving attitudes and comments suggesting that I was slightly mad or driven by some virulent form of "penis envy" (an assessment contributed by a member of the New York psychoanalytic community). Today, what I did would still be logistically complicated and challenging on many levels, but it would draw few snide remarks, and both today's young women and men would consider it a legitimate choice as long as the children were well cared for. This says a lot about how much Western societies have changed in a single generation. The old challenges may remain in others.

By extending her circle of care and concern, it is fairly easy for a woman (and any man so inclined) to slide from Center TWO past the Egoic Center THREE and adopt some of the values and worldview of the Aloha Center FOUR. However, if she lacks the gutsy self-confidence and practical realism needed to actualize these values in the world, such heartful aspirations may remain just that – unless the necessary work skills and discipline are also developed, along with confidence and appropriate assertiveness. A lack of any of these qualities could then form the substance of a return cycle to Center THREE to fill in these gaps.

It is interesting in this context to note the numbers of women and men today who are going back to school at midlife or even later to acquire skills and knowledge needed to pursue newly formulated goals, and often new careers altogether. I have also noticed that the courage to do that often comes from feeling a Star Center call in some form. Whether identified as such or not, this subtle call seems to help them recognize gaps in competencies that need to be filled and then go for it, even if it means a temporary "come-down" in status or income. A research study by Dr. Robin Seeley at the Institute of Transpersonal Psychology in California found this to be true in a group of mid-life women who were changing or newly starting careers that were deeply and personally meaningful to them.

Conversely, more men than women tend to bypass or do only the required minimum to get by at Center TWO in order to get to the Egoic Center (THREE) as fast as possible to achieve proficiency in an area that enables them to compete successfully for the social and financial rewards of money, power, and prestige. This, too, is encouraged by strong social expectations that a man do a good job of materially supporting himself and his family, as well as doing his part in the governance of the community and participating in the defense of kinship territory. This strategy may leave a deficiency in social skills and awareness, leading to interpersonal problems regardless of the level of career and/or public success attained.

Today, as gender differences are blurring, more women are also joining in this pattern, while some men, in turn, are opting out of the "rat race" in favor of a more relationship-oriented lifestyle. Yet the tendency of women to adopt circular and egalitarian rather than hierarchical ways of relating within their professional peer groups (as documented by research in the past two decades) still reflects a basically relational feminine orientation, while the warrior ethic with its power hierarchy, inherited from our mammalian past and reinforced by centuries of patriarchal value systems, is still the prevailing norm by which men are judged and judge themselves in most cultures.

The gaps in emotional and relational development left by insufficient Center TWO development tend to make the Aloha Waltz more complicated, and therefore to be a problem for more men than women. This is partly because what comes up, as we try to negotiate the transition from Power to Love, is a felt preview of the Descent Tango, but rarely with any conscious realization of what this involves, or why it is necessary. Most of the time, life has to force these learnings upon us, and sometimes the lessons are far from gentle, especially for those who have not been introspective or oriented toward psychological exploration. Women, whose focus on relationship tends to make them in general more psychologically oriented, seem to find this descent a bit easier – but I say this with caution because there are many exceptions to any such generalization.

## Resonances

Resonances are an interesting phenomenon I have observed as people move within and through the Centers, especially in the thick of the return cycles. When you strike a note on the piano, the strings of the same note across all the other octaves vibrate in sync at lower and higher frequencies – like an echo. A similar resonance seems to occur across the Centers so that, whenever one is energized, others with similar energy will also be activated. This happens most strongly along the Centers we have just explored: ONE-THREE-FIVE and TWO-FOUR-SIX.

For example, if I am contemplating a career change while centered at THREE, my ego needs are primary in determining what I will consider. Will it be a move up or down in status and prestige? Will I make more money? Will it look good on my resume? Will it impress my peers? Will I be successful at it? Survival issues are embedded in the concern about making more money, shifting my focus to Center ONE, although at a level beyond mere physical survival.

Will the new direction bring me personal satisfaction? Will it fit my talents and interests? This is a Center FIVE resonance. Although Ego-based and devoid of transpersonal aspirations of aligning with a purpose beyond self, most of the time we do also consider finding the right fit for this self in a larger social context. Sometimes this resonance is unconscious, and may manifest in inner resistance or procrastination when we face a decision that, to all intents and purposes, the Ego should eagerly embrace. We may be surprised and puzzled at our own reaction, regardless of what we actually do about it.

We may well ignore this faint echo of the Star call and go for the money and prestige, but the inexplicable unease may still persist. Sometimes this decision is necessary if a career change is driven by immediate need, as when someone with a family to support loses a job and can't pay the bills. It then becomes a survival issue, and from the perspective of Center ONE, the prime consideration is how best to earn enough to cover expenses. Resonances with the other Centers then fade into the background, though their faint echoes still remain.

In the same way, when our hearts open to the suffering of humanity and we extend ourselves to help where we can regardless of whether the recipients belong to our kinship circle or not (Center FOUR), we still make sure our dear ones are taken care of, and tend to give preference to those who feel more like "kin" than others (Center TWO). On the other hand, there is the echo of Sophia wisdom (Center SIX) reminding us that we all embody the same Spirit and share the same sufferings and have the same human needs. Thus we are all worthy of care and assistance when needed.

I don't know about resonances at Center SEVEN, but assume that it encompasses and transcends all the Centers, and resonates with them all because it represents the ground of all the phenomena described and is therefore beyond all polarities. It may well be the resonance of Center SEVEN within us at all the other Centers that prompts us to persevere on our spiritual path in the first place, or even to buy books like this as a help along the way.

## The Body on the Path

As embodied beings, everything we experience is also reflected in our bodies in some form as somatic memory. The body-heart-mind connection is an ongoing web of interdependent events reflecting our journey – for better and for worse. The more we are learning about this integral process – and there has been a quantum leap in our collective knowledge in the past two or three decades – the more we realize just how deeply and literally em-bodied we are. It is a fascinating area of study, and I have only a rudimentary and tentative understanding, but I will briefly share with you my current thoughts.

These are the kinds of body/mind connections I have come to associate with each of the Centers:

*ONE:* Undifferentiated from body; identity with the body-self. A direct, uncomplicated, self-protective response to one's world.

*TWO:* The reflected body, with its related self-image mirroring feedback from significant others and the social environment. A need for admiration and approval of one's body-self by significant others. This is where we develop personal vanity, as well as rejection of the body if it does not measure up to cultural models of attractiveness. In healthy development, we also take joy in physical movement and play, feeling pleasure in and through our body.

*THREE:* The instrumental body, which we try to mold into a form that will serve Ego's self-enhancement agenda, as in image-making and PR "packaging." Defensive or counter-aggressive response to any perceived threat to self-image.

In positive form, we develop discipline and mastery of physical skills that enhance our confidence and sense of successful agency in the world. We develop "guts."

*FOUR:* The affectionate body, reaching out toward others, accepting ourselves and others as they are. Possible neglect of our physical needs because the body is seen as less important than relatedness and caring, and we focus on and identify with the objects of our care at the expense of self-care.

*FIVE:* The expressive body, with a creative approach to our physicality and a sense of relatedness to the body as a miraculous vehicle of our growth process, with its own legitimate needs and demands and not just a servant of our personal agenda.

The lack of self-care may carry over from the Aloha Center, because we may become intensely immersed in our creative and self-expressive activities.

*SIX:* The integrated body/mind as embodiment of Spirit/Sophia. Recognition of the body's own deep wisdom, and its capacity to be our guide and disciplinarian.

We may become frustrated with the demands of our physicality and seek to "transcend" these demands.

*SEVEN:* Conscious, embodied transcendence, with full acceptance of both without identifying with either.

Fleshing out this skeletal formulation and discovering how these all interweave is a task for the future. I am only beginning to experientially understand the crucial role of immanence in spiritual development, having spent most of my life taking for granted my body and its healthy functioning in the service of my needs and wishes. It took several wake-up calls for me to pay enough attention to *its* needs – and learn to listen to *its* amazing wisdom. Therefore, the brevity of this section in no way downplays the importance of this topic, but simply reflects the degree of my own current ignorance.

I hope this will be helpful for now. A rich literature exploring body/mind interactions already exists, and I encourage you to explore it. Also, Dr. Rosemarie Anderson has been researching this connection through stages closely mirroring mine (eight stages rather than seven), and will very likely publish her findings in the near future

## Detours

We may get stuck for many reasons. The undertow of old emotions may entrap us, which is why psychological readiness, a well-functioning and compassionate inner witness, and a safe relational container for the descent cycles are all very important. Sometimes we just plain "chicken out" of the effort and risks of growth, because confronting shadow material is hard, as is developing skills left undeveloped at earlier stages. It can be embarrassing to the Ego, and dealing with this can feel like a comedown or regression. We thought we had outgrown all this, and here it is again!

Sometimes we are pulled off course by circumstances involving close relationships with others who are on a different life path and/or whose worldview is significantly different from ours. Such a gap makes mutual understanding and meaningful sharing difficult and sometimes impossible. In broadest terms, it is difficult for an "in-law" consciousness to relate comfortably to an "out-law" consciousness, and vice versa. This makes a mutually satisfying long-term relationship, especially an intimate one, challenging and perhaps untenable. The worldview and the values that matter most to each individual are likely to differ too much, and easily lead to misunderstandings and reciprocal negative judgments. It is hard, under these conditions, for either person to be fully present to the other with an open heart and mind, and this can hinder the further development of both.

When this is compounded by significant personality differences, across such dimensions as described by Jungian typology, the Enneagram, and other ways of organizing and trying to understand some of the common patterns underlying human complexity, the task of truly connecting with another at a deep level can be even more challenging. With such differences already problematic, a "Center gap" can become the *coup de grâce* that kills a relationship even where the people involved are well meaning and honestly trying their best. It makes no sense in such cases to place or take on blame. Instead, we can use such experiences to learn more about ourselves and the range of human diversity.

Even if two people started at a similar point on the journey, if one person is on a vertical trajectory of spiritual development and the other on a more psychological or practical path of extensive horizontal development, such a gap can widen over time and become problematic because the two individuals are moving farther and farther apart in their thinking and priorities. It can be tempting to try to bridge that gap artificially by altering our own path to fit the other's, but this does not ultimately serve either person.

Another way to sabotage our journey is spiritual bypass, which we have already discussed as a serious potential pitfall on the psycho-spiritual path. Shopping for an "expressway to enlightenment" is a special and deceptive form of getting stuck, one that can easily tempt us in today's unprecedented rainbow of available spiritual paths and practices. At times it may actually seem to work if we can insulate ourselves sufficiently from those pesky "trailers" we are running away from, but they tend to catch up with us eventually, especially if and when we do try to genuinely open ourselves to new learning. At some point we will all be asked to use relational or work skills we have never mastered, or challenged with situations demanding more equanimity than we can muster, or have to deal with our old companions: fear, anger, cravings, jealousy, feelings of inadequacy, and so on. All of these need skillful handling if we are to say "Yes" to this life and live it fully, not just for Ego-enhancement but to benefit our fellow beings and leave the world at least a little better for our having passed through. So why not embrace whatever arises and respond to it as best we can, like a lucid dream we can improve upon but also know we will wake up from? We can try to be fully present to it all, to the full extent that we are able, rather than trying to "rise above it all" in ungrounded "spirituality."

And finally, there is the most common and debilitating stuckness of all: inertia. Whether out of fear, laziness, or lack of hope and purpose, some of us find a comfortable, undemanding niche in life and never move more than a very safe distance from this stable, well-worn nest, even if the inner Seed is audibly calling and life is insistently whacking us with two-by-fours to get our attention. In my clinical practice, I have seen a lot of this, but what moves some people toward growth no matter what obstacles arise in their way, and keeps others committed to a stable but familiar misery rather than exert even a little effort beyond their habitual comfort zone, remains a mystery to me.

# CHAPTER NINE

# FINAL THOUGHTS

We all have in us this capacity for wonder,
this ability to break the bonds of ordinary awareness and
sense that though our lives are fleeting and transitory,
we are part of something larger, eternal and unchanging.

Philip Simmons, *Learning to Fall*

All the return cycles aim toward psycho-spiritual integration, which involves maintaining vertical and horizontal balance as much as possible, so that, with each step toward embodied wholeness and ultimate realization, we take with us the fullest human development of which we are capable at that time. The idea of conscious development, of carrying the injunction "Know Thyself" into a serious psycho-spiritual practice, includes leaving as few trailers behind as possible. This will also make the return cycles less an archaeological dig or housecleaning, and more an experience of creative integration or even celebration.

Proceeding mindfully, trusting our own heart and intuition, at a pace that does not strain our ability to absorb and integrate our learning and experience along the way, will make getting stuck less likely, but life rarely follows such a sensible plan. Sometimes it spontaneously turns in unexpected directions, or surges forward and we get swept along, our only options being to either flow with it or resist, which is ultimately futile – just another way to get stuck. As my son put it after reading this manuscript, "I guess the greatest derailment on the path to enlightenment is not turning when the road does."

There can be illusory security but no happiness in hanging on to what we have outgrown, because a part of us always hears the call of the Seed, and failed (or rejected) transitions can be tragic. Depression often accompanies such a missed opportunity in those of us who have clearly heard Spirit's call to let go of our inner and/or outer status quo in favor of something new – and refused. The reasons for refusal may seem valid and reasonable at the time, but the effects can manifest across a wide range of psychopathology and damage our personal lives and careers.

Our basic choice is to have the humility and courage to grow and open to life – or stagnate. Even if stagnation is the logical, socially endorsed course, stagnation is still stagnation, a gilded veneer notwithstanding.

How, then, do we recognize what is trying to unfold in us? How do we know where we are called, especially if we are not used to deep introspection? This is a question I have been asked many times, and I don't have an easy answer. There are some signs, however, that seem to point toward a direction worth considering. Many of us have memories that still glow for us across time, perhaps from when we were very young and not yet thoroughly socialized. These may point to something belonging to the Seed that we may have lost or forgotten along the way. Perhaps recovering what fascinated us then, or brought us joy, will revive those feelings and enliven our present life and work.

Recurring dream themes over the years, especially the "big dreams" we never forget because of how deeply they affected us at the time, are often inner reminders of something we may want to explore. Working with dreams can be a very productive way to discover what is taking shape in our minds and possibly seeking to manifest in daily life.

What our body spontaneously opens to, what our breath and heart expand toward, can be another sign, from an embodied wisdom that bypasses our rational thinking and preconceived notions. For example, we have all met people with whom our bodies and our breath relax, and others whose presence tightens our muscles and generates an impulse to withdraw. We feel good with one, and uneasy with another. Sometimes we may even get an inexplicable feeling of utter certainty about something or someone, whether or not it makes rational sense, or whether or not we decide to act on it. This is not necessarily a comment about the other person, though sometimes it can be, especially when we sense danger. More likely, it reflects our awareness of compatible or incompatible energies, which we sense but may not recognize consciously. It is worth paying attention to these signals, without necessarily jumping to conclusions without further information and discernment.

Last but not least, I have found synchronicities to be very useful signs of whether I am on the right path or not. These meaningful "coincidences" seem to come in bunches whenever I am in harmony with the greater Flow of my life, making choices that feel authentic and Star-guided rather than coming from fear, grasping, aversion, or "shoulds." Many others have described the same experience. It is as though the outer world mirrors and supports inner authenticity, and somehow sets up roadblocks on a path that is not right for us. Pay attention and see if this fits your experience.

For much of my life I only discovered the useful guidance offered by such "signs" in retrospect, after ignoring them and making a "practical" or "logical" choice to do what I "should" or to please another. Trusting ourselves to recognize and follow our own authentic path requires both courage and self-knowledge, which are a fruit of psycho-spiritual maturation that is in turn a fruit of experiential knowledge gained through trial and error: missing the mark enough times to know where the "bull's eye" is.

All of us have our particular strand in the tapestry of creation to co-create. In this lifetime, we may be one of the barely visible background threads while others form the color and definition of the foreground design. Or we may be highly visible. Some threads are vivid and dramatic, others are subtle and serve as the backdrop against which the dramatic forms stand out better. All are needed, and any missing strand will detract from the integrity of the tapestry. So there is no reason to bemoan our place in the scheme of things. We all get to play different roles on-stage some of the time, and support the smooth flowing of the play from backstage at other times. The important thing is to listen for our cues, know what our true task is, do it to the best of our ability, and be fully present where we are, *now*.

Only we humans can aspire to be something we are not and sometimes appear to pull it off. The danger in this is losing ourselves behind the mask we create, and starting to believe that is who we are. The only thing we can successfully be is who we really are, and that is always first-rate. You are an original. Only you can be *you*, and you can't be someone else. If you try, you will always be only a copy – a counterfeit. The future is forming now, and each one of us is invited to contribute a strand to its evolving tapestry. Every single strand is important. Every thread is necessary for the completion of the design. And any strand can modify the whole, if only a little.

Remember that we are most deeply spiritual when we are most deeply and authentically ourselves, because in our essence we are, by definition, spiritual beings – having a human experience, as the saying goes. This has several implications:

1. We do not have to become *different* to be spiritual. In fact, we don't have to *become* spiritual – we already *are*.

2. The spiritual journey is not *going* anywhere, but is rather a cyclical inner process of peeling off the layers of conditioning and inauthenticity obscuring our true essence – letting *that* shine through the fog of mentally created confusion and manifest its unique beauty in the realm of matter and mind. The Greeks called this manifestation Sophia, and it is a life's journey to find her where she lives, in ourselves. Love, as natural quality and expression of Wisdom, embodies as Sophia. This is what we all seek, relentlessly and so often unknowingly, because this is our deepest Essence, which was always there.

I really like the metaphor of us all as water in the vastness of the same infinite ocean. As water in perpetual flux, aren't we all essentially waves of that endlessly pulsing ocean? Yet each wave, as a temporary and unique coherent impulse arising from water, is unique in its details and distinct from every other wave. It exists and has real power only as long as it continues to move forward, and ends by dissolving again into quiescence, no longer distinguishable from the ocean. To deeply know the essence of water in one wave, or even one drop, is to know the essence of water anywhere in that ocean.

The difficulty in making models and conceptual distinctions is that everything that arises from the eternal Ground eventually returns to It, and so whenever we create categories and models as though they were enduring realities, we also fixate and falsify something that is in constant evolutionary flux. Conceptual models are useful as a framework and/or map in negotiating this flux, and it is a human decision where to make the appropriate "cut" for the purpose it is designed to serve. This model constitutes such a cut — a perspective on the ocean from the crest of one wave.

It is obvious that no one model can fully describe the human journey, any more than any map tells us everything about the territory it represents, but by highlighting major roadways and topographical features, a map remains useful in keeping our bearings and being aware of what to look for on the way. I hope this "map" has given you a useful framework to make sense of your own unique life's journey, as you explore the richness of your psycho-spiritual development in the only place it is to be found: your own first-hand experience.

Remember to hold all conceptual models lightly and trust yourself. Also, question yourself. Do I see more clearly when I look at my world through this lens? Does it give me more insight? Does it add meaning to my life? If so, may you use your insights wisely, and may the light of Sophia always grow and shine through you in ever-expanding ripples of Aloha.

# ACKNOWLEDGMENTS

Many midwives assisted in the birth of this book, and I want to thank them all, starting with the ITP students and colleagues who responded enthusiastically to this model as first presented, especially Professors Rosemarie Anderson, William Braud, Bob Frager, and Bob Schmidt, in whose class it was first articulated.

Strong encouragement to develop it further also came from many students, friends, and participants at the workshops I subsequently offered, as well as readers of the article published in 1997, some e-mailed from distant parts of the world.

There are others I specifically want to thank. Sandy Hastings provided friendship, constant practical support, and feedback when needed, as did Genie Palmer, whose ongoing use of the model with dissertation students convinced me of its usefulness. Berkeley Fuller volunteered his computer mastery to create the first poster used in the early workshops and then the article. Hal Bennett provided both professional advice and friendly nudging to persevere with the book, and Jill Mellick was generous with her artistic insight when I was struggling with its graphic representation.

As I was trying to articulate what for me did not initially come in words or concepts, ongoing dialogue with a number of people brought greater clarity. Rosemarie Anderson provided ongoing in-depth dialogue; Beverly Gorsuch served as a psycho-spiritual mirror and inspiration; William Braud read the first draft and provided insightful comments; Cydria Manette gave me her writer's insights and encouragement; Dolores and Bob Scheelen pointed to ways to improve clarity for the reader. Bob Frager's response to the draft convinced me that it was time to publish and stop tinkering with details. I thank them all, and others who also helped along the way.

As the birth neared, the consummate artistic and computer skills of Marcia O'Rourke gave the actual book its form. She is responsible for creating the cover, formatting of the book, and the colorful graphic depiction of the pathways through the seven Centers. Her creativity amazes me.

A very special thank you, with much love, goes to my two children: Michael Kroon, copy editor extraordinaire, whose accuracy of language puts me to shame and whose keen insights from the viewpoint of someone outside the fields of psychology and spirituality helped to sharpen many passages of the text; and Dominique Sukles, whose loving support and personal interest in the model led to valuable feedback and further clarifications and examples which I would not have otherwise thought to include. I also thank them both for their friendship and eternal bemused tolerance of a mother who never quite fit the usual maternal image.

For the inner confidence to finally complete this project, and for so much more, I am deeply grateful to my spiritual teacher and mentor, Lama Surya Das, whose example, guidance, and inspiration are beacons on my own ongoing Journey.

And last but by no means least, thank you to all those who, over the years, allowed me to walk with them on their life journey and share their inner world. Without you, this book would not exist.

I send you all my heartfelt *Aloha*.

# ABOUT THE AUTHOR

Hillevi Ruumet is a transpersonal psychologist rooted in the tradition and discoveries of C. G. Jung, with an undergraduate degree from Mount Holyoke College and a Ph.D. in Clinical Psychology from Columbia University.

She taught and practiced psychotherapy for three decades in varied roles – as member of a hospital psychiatry department, in independent private practice of psychotherapy and consulting, as a pioneering workshop leader in stress management and holistic lifestyle promotion, and as full time core faculty at the Institute of Transpersonal Psychology in Palo Alto, California, with special responsibilities as director of clinical training. She remains on the ITP faculty as an adjunct research professor.

Dr. Ruumet is also an ecumenically trained spiritual director. The psycho-spiritual "map" presented in this book is an extension of *Pathways of the Soul: A Helical Model of Psychospiritual Development*, an article published in *Presence: The Journal of Spiritual Directors International* in September, 1997. Since then, she has taught the model in a number of workshops, and this book was written largely in response to requests by readers and workshop participants.

Now living in Southern Oregon, she continues her spiritual journey and practice in semi-retirement, as she shares her lifetime of learning through writing, giving periodic workshops and public presentations, and consulting with individuals regarding their psycho-spiritual development and practice.

Printed in the United States
By Bookmasters